CALL TO AMERICA
TO BUILD ZION

This is a volume in the Arno Press collection

AMERICA AND THE HOLY LAND

Advisory Editor
Professor Moshe Davis

Editorial Board
Professor Robert Theodore Handy
Professor Jules Davids
Dr. Nathan M. Kaganoff

America-Holy Land Studies
A Joint Project of the
American Jewish Historical Society
David R. Pokross, President

Dr. Maurice Jacobs, Chairman
of the American Jewish Historical Society-Institute
of Contemporary Jewry Liaison Committee
and the
Institute of Contemporary Jewry
The Hebrew University of Jerusalem
Dr. Daniel G. Ross, Chairman
of the Institute's International Planning Committee

See last pages of this volume for a complete list of titles.

CALL TO AMERICA
TO BUILD ZION

ARNO PRESS

A New York Times Company

New York / 1977

Editorial Supervision: JOSEPH CELLINI

Reprint Edition 1977 by Arno Press Inc.

Copyright © 1977 by Arno Press Inc.

Discourse on the Restoration of the Jews and Zionism in Prophecy were reprinted from copies in the American Jewish Historical Society Library.

AMERICA AND THE HOLY LAND
ISBN for complete set: 0-405-10220-8
See last pages of this volume for titles.

Manufactured in the United States of America

Library of Congress Cataloging in Publication Data

Main entry under title:

Call to America to build Zion.

(America and the Holy Land)
 Reprint of the 1814 ed. of Isaiah's message to the American nation, by J. McDonald, printed by E. & E. Hosford, Albany; the 1845 ed. of Discourse on the restoration of the Jews, by M. M. Noah, published by Harper, New York; and the 1936 ed. of Zionism in prophecy, distributed by Pro-Palestine Federation of America, New York.
 1. Jews--Restoration--Addresses, essays, lectures. 2. Bible. O. T. Isaiah XVIII--Commentaries. 3. Grand Island, N. Y.--Addresses, essays, lectures. 4. Zionism--Addresses, essays, lectures. I. Bible. O. T. Isaiah XVIII. English. 1814. McDonald. 1977. II. Noah, Mordecai Manuel, 1785-1851. Discourse on the restoration of the Jews. 1977. III. Title: Zionism in prophecy. 1977. IV. Series.
BS649.J5C34   296.3   77-70723
ISBN 0-405-10306-9

In tribute to
DANIEL G. ROSS
for his leadership, friendship and counsel

CONTENTS

McDonald, John
ISAIAH'S MESSAGE TO THE AMERICAN NATION: A New Translation, of Isaiah, Chapter XVIII, With Notes Critical and Explanatory. Albany, 1814

Noah, M[ordecai] M[anuel]
DISCOURSE ON THE RESTORATION OF THE JEWS: Delivered at the Tabernacle, Oct. 28 and Dec. 2, 1844. New York, 1845

ZIONISM IN PROPHECY: The Return of Israel to the Holy Land; A Fulfillment of Biblical Promises. [New York], 1936

A

NEW TRANSLATION,

OF

ISAIAH, CHAPTER XVIII.

WITH

NOTES CRITICAL AND EXPLANATORY,

A REMARKABLE PROPHECY, RESPECTING THE *RESTORATION OF THE JEWS*,
AIDED BY THE *AMERICAN NATION*;

WITH

AN UNIVERSAL SUMMONS TO THE *BATTLE OF ARMAGEDDON*, AND A
DESCRIPTION OF THAT SOLEMN SCENE.

BY JOHN McDONALD, A. M.
Pastor of the Presbyterian Church, in Chapel-Street, Albany.

―――Si quid novisti rectius istis :
Candidus imperti : si non, his utere mecum.   *Hor. Epist. Lib.* 3—6.

ALBANY :
PRINTED BY E. & E. HOSFORD.

1814.

INTRODUCTION.

Of all the Jewish prophets, Isaiah holds the most distinguished place. His predictions embrace subjects of great variety, extent and importance, and he delivers them with an elegance and energy peculiarly his own. In him the richest vein of poetic genius is united to an uncommon portion of the spirit of inspiration.

With great propriety he stiles his revelations from God, visions; for Jehovah, not only addressed his ear, but delineated the scenes themselves with all their agents, colouring and circumstances, and presented them to his eye. He continued to prophecy the greater part of an hundred years, and has unfolded a prophetic history of the church of God till the consummation of all things.

Interesting, however, as his communications are, and though in general written with great perspicuity, there is no portion of scripture that presents, in several instances, difficulties more serious to the Theological student. These arise, from the vast variety of his subjects: from his rapid and abrupt transitions: from the sudden and unexpected change of the speakers: from his bold and figurative diction: from the paucity of the historical records of the nations that he introduces: from the numerous verbal errors, which through the carelessness of transcribers have crept into the original text :—from obscurity in translation.

The prophecy which we have ventured to translate and offer to the public, with some explanatory observations, has been universally acknowledged as the least intelligible in the whole collection. No two translators, no two commentators are completely agreed in their application of it.

Lowth, sometime Bishop of London, a distinguished Hebrew scholar and scripture critic, who, has given an elegant translation of Isaiah, with valuable annotations, begins his notes on this chapter, in these words: " This is one of the

INTRODUCTION.

"most obscure prophecies in the whole book of Isaiah. The
"subject of it—the end and design of it—the people to whom it
"is addressed—the history to which it belongs—the person who
"sends—the messengers and the nation to whom the ambassadors
"are sent, are all obscure and doubtful."

Since the publication of the Bishop's translation, the study of the prophecies and of sacred criticism, has been conducted on principles and with an ardour, formerly unknown. Faber, Fraser, and others, have laboured with credit and success. Providence in recent astonishing events and revolutions, is daily furnishing illustrations on this subject.

Horsley, late Bishop of St. Asaph, a scholar and critic of a superior order, dissatisfied with the common translations of this prophecy, gave a new version accompanied with notes. These he published in a letter, and Faber, with just encomiums has since added the translation and notes, to the second volume of his dissertations on the prophecies. Horsley with his *Ithuriel spear* smites this sealed vision, the seals burst open, and for the first time revealed, tho' obscurely, the real treasure. Impatience or other avocations prevented that importunate interrogation to which alone prophecy will listen.

Commencing a course of morning lectures on Isaiah, upwards of two years ago, the author soon discovered that his knowledge of its contents was beyond conception limited and obscure. Recourse for aid, to such commentators as lay within his reach, convinced him that they were far from being enlightened and satisfactory guides. Diffuse where they might have been silent; and silent where difficulty and darkness prevailed. Even Calvin, the most judicious of that class, very frequently illustrates his Theological system, where he ought to give, and we expect his exposition of the prophecy.

Disappointed in himself and in his aids, he determined to become his own translator, and to keep a steady eye on the prophet, in his manner as well as in his expression. Unless under the influence of self deception, a case not very uncommon, he views his labour and patience amply repaid.

On his first approach to this chapter he found it enveloped in darkness impenetrable. Every attempt to discover its meaning was fruitless. He left it sealed as he found it.

INTRODUCTION.

Several months elapsed, before a ray of light fell upon it. In the close of the prophecies, and especially in the last chapter, phrases similar to those in this prophecy frequently occurred. He found that they all had a reference to that awful day with which God shall terminate the present, and introduce a more glorious dispensation.

Under these impressions, he returned and began to apply the contents of this chapter to the same event, and the application appeared natural and satisfactory. Horsley's translation, about the same time, falling in his way, added confidence to his own conjecture. He resolved to publish the result of his enquiries, as they appear related to a scene, on which the present aspect of providence seems to invite the public eye. The view of the prophecy as here exhibited, is calculated to press on the American mind the important part which Heaven has destined our nation to act in this wonderful drama. Pious students in Theology it is hoped may also be stirred up to prepare themselves or their successors to undertake the divine embassy to which God will call them in his providence, as he now calls them in his prophecy.

The author relies, in confidence, on the candour and indulgence of those best qualified to judge of the subject with its evidence and the execution.

In a first attempt on a subject both difficult and delicate, where alterations and corrections—not always improvements, are constantly taking place, smoothness and uniformity of stile cannot be preserved, nor is it possible entirely to exclude ambiguity in expression and grammatical violation.

ISAIAH, Chap. XVIII.

GENERAL VIEW OF THE CHAPTER.

1. God calls aloud on the American nation—her situation and national characteristics described—sheltered under the out spread wings of her own eagle—placed beyond the rivers of Cush, at that time the western boundary of Jewish Geographical knowledge—sending ambassadors by sea and in vessels of reeds on the face of her own waters. 2. A commission given to her gospel messengers, represented as qualified and prepared to carry her message to the dispersion of Jacob—his description of this people—scattered—plundered—subjected to terror in the extreme—of marvellous expectation—in deep oppression, whose country is in complete desolation. 3. A summons to all the inhabitants of the world on seeing the standard unfurled and hearing the sound of the trumpet to prepare and hasten to the battle of God. 4. Jehovah's private message to the prophet, stating the nature of his providential dispensation till the time of the battle. 5. A prophetic vision of the battle under the similitude of the destruction of a vineyard on the very eve of vintage. 6. A view of the field of battle, with the armies and their principal leader, abandoned unburied, to birds and beasts of prey. 7. The American nation, uniting with the friends of Christ of all nations, in presenting the Jews wonderfully changed, as an oblation to God of the first fruits of men, in Mount Zion.

ISAIAH, CHAP. XVIII.

Common Translation.	*New Translation.*
1. Woe to the land shadowing with wings, which is beyond the rivers of Ethiopia.	1. Ho! the land of the overshadowing wings, that lies beyond the rivers of Cush.
2. That sendeth ambassadors by the sea, even in vessels of bulrushes upon the waters, *saying,* Go, ye swift messengers, to a nation scattered and peeled, to a people terrible from their beginning hitherto; a nation meted out and trodden down, whose land the rivers have spoiled!	2. That sendeth ambassadors by sea, and in vessels of reeds on the face of the waters. Swift messengers, go ye to a nation, dispersed and pillaged, to a people under terror in the very extreme, a nation of expectation, of expectation and trodden down, whose country rivers have spoiled!

ISAIAH, CHAP. XVIII.

Common Translation.

3. All ye inhabitants of the world, and dwellers on the earth, see ye, when he lifteth up an ensign on the mountains; and when he bloweth a trumpet, hear ye.

4. For so the LORD said to me, I will take my rest, and I will consider in my dwelling place like a clear heat upon herbs, *and* like a cloud of dew in the heat of harvest.

5. For afore the harvest, when the bud is perfect, and the sour grape is ripening in the flower, he shall both cut off the sprigs with pruning hooks, and take away *and* cut down the branches.

6. They shall be left together unto the fowls of the mountains, and to the beasts of the earth: and the fowls shall summer on them, and all the beasts of the earth shall winter on them.

7. ¶ In that time shall the season be brought unto the LORD of hosts of a people scattered and peeled, and from a people terrible from their beginning hitherto; a nation meted out and trodden under foot, whose land the rivers have spoiled, to the place of the name of LORD of hosts, the mount Zion.

New Translation.

3. All ye inhabitants of the world, and all ye that dwell on earth, when the standard is lifted upon the mountains, look ye! and when the trumpet is sounded listen ye!

4. Then thus did JEHOVAH say to me: I will sit still now and I will look intently from my habitation, like serene heat after bright sunshine, and like a dewy cloud in the heat of harvest.

5. But while the harvest was passing away, when the bud had become perfect, and the blossom had changed into the juicy grape: he cut down the luxuriant branches with pruning hooks: he removed the standard vine: he cut in pieces!

6. They abandon them promiscuously to the eagle of the mountains, and to the beasts of the field. On HIM the eagle of the mountains is glutted; even on HIM all the beasts of the field insultingly riot!

7. At that time shall a present be brought to JEHOVAH of hosts, of a people dispersed and pillaged, even of a people under terror in the very extreme, a nation of expectation, of expectation and trodden down, whose country rivers have spoiled—to the place of the name of JEHOVAH of hosts—mount Zion

VERSE 1.

"Ho! the land of the overshadowing wings that lieth beyond the "rivers of Cush, that sendeth ambassadors by sea and in vessels "of reeds on the face of the waters."

NOTES AND ILLUSTRATIONS.

In this verse, JEHOVAH addresses, in the hearing of the prophet, a distant country, of which it is probable he submitted to his view, a prophetic landscape. The prophet reports what he heard and saw.

ISAIAH, CHAP. XVIII. V. 1.

Ho ! the land.] This is an earnest claim on her attention, and not as, in our translation, an imprecation. The scope and spirit of the address breathes nothing but friendship and confidence. In this sense it is employed by the prophet himself, chap. lv. 1. " Ho every one that thirsteth, come ye to the waters." The word in the original is employed in scripture, to give utterance to any violent agitation of mind, excited by apprehension of danger or produced by strong aversion or desire.

Land of the overshadowing wings.] This is evidently designed, to point out a country, distinguished by the appendage of wings, either literal or metaphorical. Persons and places, are frequently represented in scripture by some of their appropriate qualities. Pharoah, in allusion to the Crocodile of his Nile is called the Dragon of the river. The princes of Moab are called Bulls of Bashan, on account of the distinguished breed of cattle that were reared in that noble district. Alexander of Macedon, from his nerve in exertion, from his caprice, and from the rapidity of his motions, guided more by love of fame than by thirst of blood, is stiled by Daniel, the HE GOAT of Macedonia. Our Saviour describes the Roman armies, by eagles, from the figure of that bird which decorated their marching Legions, their battles and their camp. Rome, because built on seven celebrated hills is named the beast with seven heads. Guided by these analogies we may fairly infer, that the country addressed will probably be distinguished, by a bird with wide spreading wings painted on her national standards, or by the features of the country, which in the vision met the prophets eye and awakened his poetic imagination.

Near the close of the eighteenth century, a nation emerged on the eastern shore of the American continent, that chose an eagle with expanded wings for her national ensign. The Persian conqueror and the Roman Republic, adopted the same bird to distinguish their respective standards. But their eagles represented that winged bird in hostile attitude, and eager for the prey. The American eagle, without one unfriendly feature, extends her wings for the protection of her own nation, and offers a shelter for the persecuted of all the nations of the earth. Armed on one side with the branch of peace extended, and on the other with the weapons of her aborigines, she is prepared for defence and no-

B

for aggression. Happy nation didst thou understand the language of this emblem, and didst thou follow its instruction! The standard and the genius of the nation happily harmonize. History records no other government, that has been established solely for the protection of the governed, and the refuge of the stranger. America is the only nation on earth that invites persons of all countries, of all languages, of all religions, of all complexions, habits and manners, to repair to her standard, to settle on her soil, and to share without degrading distinctions, in all her invaluable privileges. Other nations, almost without exception, dread, hate and repel the stranger, and instead of presenting the *olive* and the *wing*, meet them with the spear and the sword.

That our application of this epithet to the American nation, is in strict analogy to other predictions of the same prophet already accomplished, will appear from his celebrated description of Cyrus, chap. xlvi. 10, 11. God had appointed him by prophecy as the scourge of Babylon and the deliverer of the captive Jews. He produces this decree as proof of his knowledge and fore ordination of all future events. " My counsel shall stand and I " will do all my pleasure, calling from the east an *eagle*, the *man* " that executeth my counsel from a far country." *Ravenous bird*, the English version is the description, instead of the name of the bird. *Eagle*, makes the inspired prophecy exactly agree with Xenophon the Grecian biographer of Cyrus. The historian in his 7th book, informs us, that when the conqueror entered on this expedition he ordered a golden eagle to be elevated as the standard of his army, and under it he destroyed Babylon. The Persian and Hebrew name of this bird is " aët" and so scrupulous is the historian that he retains the name with the addition of the Greek termination *os*. making it *äetos*. No one will deny that the prediction referred to Cyrus, and was fulfilled in him. It may with confidence be asked, can *the overshadowing wing*, when applied to America, be less intelligible than *eagle*, when applied to Cyrus? Time has rendered the one clear as demonstration : time is gradually enlightening the other.

Were it possible, that the eye of the American patriot, who first suggested the adoption of the eagle, as the ensign of his country, or even those who concurred in the device, should meet and approve of these remarks, astonishment and serious reflection must be excited. Full and frank must be their acknowledgment, that with no more knowledge of the prophecy of JEHOVAH, or of intention of fulfilling it, their selection was made, than Cyrus had, when, from accidental suggestion, he constructed his golden eagle.

Land beyond the rivers of Cush.] This part of the description ascertains the situation and distance of the country addressed. Cush was the eldest son of Ham. His descendants appear in the tenth chapter of Genesis, to have occupied the regions round ancient Babylon, on the streams of the Euphrates, and soon after the flood, became numerous and powerful. At a very early period not recorded in history, a colony of this family emigrated, and settled on the shores of the Arabian Gulf, and on the waters of the Upper Nile, and were known in scripture by the appellation of Cushites; but by the Greeks and Romans, they were called Ethiopians.

Meroe, surrounded by the waters of the Nile, the *Atapas* and the *Astobaros*, their capital city, lay south west of Jerusalem, and in the days of Isaiah, terminated on the west the geographical knowledge of the Jews, and by them was accounted the ends of the earth.

On passing these rivers, the most extensive and frightful desart in the world commences, and continues without intermission for nearly three thousand miles, till it reaches the shores of the Atlantic. In that immense ocean of sand, no civilized nation, no commercial streams, ever did, or can exist. Beyond this, in the same direction then, this winged nation must be sought.

Guided by the prospective view of the prophet, we pass the wide Atlantic wave. On reaching its western shore, a new and then unknown world is discovered.

From each side of a narrow Isthmus, resembling a neck, two vast continents stretch, to the frozen regions of the south, and the north. They resemble the wings of a bird. Ridges of central mountains, covered with lofty forests, like variegated plumage, extend almost to their extremities. In front, and almost connected with the continent, the West-India Islands, decked in all their tropic colours, like the decorated head of a bird, project and meet the eye. Sheltered under the northern, and most expansive wing of this gigantic Bird, the American nation bursts on the view, bearing on her standard, her Eagle, emblem of the profile of her hemisphere, and of the genius of her government.

On a slight inspection of a common map of America, without much aid from fancy, the resemblance will appear. But when God drew the landscape, with all its features, and in all the glowing tints of light and shade, and presented it to the vivid imagination of the sacred Poet, must he not have re-echoed ; *Land of the overshadowing wings !* Can we on listening to the description and comparing it with America, withhold exclaiming: It is the picture of our own country, painted by our own God !

Which sendeth Ambassadors by sea.] This is the third descriptive feature in the character of the country, that JEHOVAH addresses. The term ambassador, as *Bp.* Horsley observes, includes commercial as well as political agents. America, is distinguished for the number of the agents that she employs in both capacities. Every other nation, ancient or modern with whose history or manners we are acquainted, could, and actually did, send their ambassadors by land. The ancient Romans and Carthagenians, the British, the Danes, and others of the same description, furnish no exceptions. They sent ambassadors over narrow arms of the sea only, a passage generally performed in the space of a few hours. Recent attempts of the British and French, to send ambassadors by sea, to China, proved unsuccessful, and had they succeeded, they might have been sent by land.

America is the only nation on earth, which cannot send her ambassadors to any civilized, or commercial nation, or state, but by sea. She is constantly dispatching ambassadors to various countries, in this channel. She has hardly attained the thirtieth year of her national existence, and in the number of her ambassadors, she is scarcely exceeded by the oldest and most powerful nations of the world.

And in vessels of reeds, on the face of the waters.] This is the fourth and last discriminating characteristic of this distant nation. The preceding respected her commerce with foreign nations; this regards the manner of internal intercourse among her own citizens.

No country in the world is more favoured with navigable waters for light vessels, than America; and none of equal population, employs them in greater number on the face of their streams. Her rivers with their various ramifications, spread over the face of the whole country, and visit every corner of her extensive territory. In every direction we find the boatman wafting the produce of her soil, to her different emporiums. Her inland seas, sufficiently capacious and deep, to float the largest navies of the globe, are with their tributary streams, wonderfully extensive and intimately connected with each other. Majestic, as her rivers and lakes are, they are rendered inaccessible in a great measure to every foreign sail. This will perpetuate and increase her internal navigation, and secure to her the name of the country of the Canoe, through future ages.

Vessels of reeds.] In Egypt, whose canals were shallow and her rivers rapid, vessels of reeds were constructed to surmount these impediments. Isaiah had probably seen these vessels, or at least had heard them described. In his vision, when he saw the American waters, covered with her bark canoes, and light batteaux, which so much resembled the vessels of the Nile, he calls them by the same name—vessels of Bulrushes.

The whole of the American land, from the St. Lawrence to the Mississippi, and from the ocean to Ontario, and her sister lakes, exhibits her numerous waters, all alive by the number and variety of her swift sailing vessels. This species of communication is in rapid growth, and the time is probably not far distant when her statesmen, her judges, her merchants and her travellers, shall employ no other vehicle, to convey them to their seats of legislation, of justice and of commerce.

Of all the nations and states that have risen, and flourished, and sunk for the space of twenty-five hundred years, to none of them can the preceding marks be applied with propriety. All expositors acknowledge this. To the American nation, every one of them may be applied with an aptitude, the most astonishing and exact. The nation addressed must be America. The proof which it furnishes for the truth of prophecy, is new and beautiful. The prescience of God, in events and circumstances the most minute and apparently the most fortuitous, ought to appal the heart of the most obstinate infidel, and dispose him to yield to evidence so clear;—it ought to confirm the confidence and faith of every pious believer!

VERSE 2.

" Swift messengers, Go ye to a nation, dispersed and plunder-
" ed, to a people in terror in the extreme, a nation of expectation,

"of expectation and trodden down, whose country, rivers have
"spoiled."

NOTES AND ILLUSTRATIONS.

Here a new scene is introduced. Without any previous notice or explanation, Jehovah abruptly withdraws the eye and attention of the prophet from the country and its description, and directs them to a more interesting subject. Persons in the habit and attitude of messengers, present themselves prepared and ready to receive the charge, and commission of their King. In the hearing and view of the prophet, he addresses them in these solemn and rapid accents!

Swift Messengers, Go ye.] Angels or messengers, the epithet in the text, is employed in scripture to designate, agents dispatched by God, from heaven with messages of mercy to men, or those ministers of religion whom he qualifies and calls to instruct sinners in the way of salvation. Messengers of the former kind were frequently sent to Abraham, and to Jacob, to prophets and apostles in every age. By this name also, our Saviour, in each of his letters to the Asiatic churches, addresses their respective Pastors or Bishops. Christ himself, when in the execution of his prophetical office, is called also by the same name. Malachi, when closing the canon of the Old Testament, promises Christ, and his forerunner, under this appellation. " Behold I will send my mes-
" senger, and he shall prepare the way before me; and JEHOVAH,
" whom ye seek shall suddenly come to his temple, the messenger
" of the covenant in whom ye delight."

The persons who receive the charge in the text, we may therefore conclude, are American Clergymen, whom God by his grace shall qualify, and in his providence raise up, for engaging in a work, on which his heart has long been set. Blessed are they, who shall be called!

In some parts of this prophecy, a call is given to particular nations in the eastern hemisphere, to engage in this service, Isa. lx.—4.—10. In other places the whole world is represented as united in the same cause, chap. lxvi. 19, 20. Among these no doubt the American nation was included.

But God delights to distinguish his last born nation, and the youngest of Zion's daughters, with special tokens of regard. To her he devotes a whole prophecy, sends her a separate message, and delivers the commission to her Angels, by his own mouth. Once by regal tyranny and prelatical intolerance and pride, she was in her infancy separated from all the nations and churches on earth, and driven for shelter to the very ends of the world. God in holy retribution, shall remember the sons of the pilgrims, and shall, in the *last days* bestow on them separate honors.

Nation and churches of New-England, cradle and nurse of the American churches, exert yourselves with your learned and venerable Pastors, to train up messengers for God! By your influence, and by multiplying your prayers, prepare your sons and your posterity by your exertions, as legions of angels to unite with your Redeemer, in bringing back to him, his kindred according to the flesh!

Already the nations of Europe are awake, and preparing for that eventful hour. Denmark to her immortal honour has taken the lead in preparing and sending forth missionaries of talents, prudence and zeal. Britain follows with exertions more vigorous, corresponding to her numbers, opulence and zeal. America has also engaged in this holy cause. Missionary and Bible societies, executing translations into numerous languages, rapidly increase. From the remote inland seas of America, they already extend to the frozen wilds of Siberia. Emperors, princes, nobles, and an innumerable host of the untitled pious, unite and give support and countenance to this heaven delighting work!

The study of the prophecies, a sure sign of the approach of some important revolution in the religious world, is prosecuted with unusual ardour and success. When our Daniels set their hearts to understand the prophecies, deliverance may be expected as near.

A new and unaccountable impulse has recently been communicated to Hebrew students. This study flourishes in Europe, and young American Clergymen of every denomination, have recently turned their attention with ardour, to this venerable language. Hebrew literature, accompanied with an intimate acquaintance with prophecy, may be considered as the best external accomplishments for Jewish missionaries. To these let burning zeal, and charitable and holy affections be added, with disinterested generosity, and we may soon expect the downfall of Jewish infidelity—Jerusalem inhabited—and Zion rising from the dust in more than primeval splendor.

Swift.] The import of this epithet, it is not easy, perhaps it is impossible yet accurately to ascertain. It is probable from the spirit of the text, that the call will be instantaneous and at a season when the circumstances of the Jews, shall have become critical. Speed and exertion will then become absolutely necessary, and that in a high degree.

It may have a special reference to the ardour and external accomplishments of the missionaries. They shall partake of the spirit of the primitive preachers of the gospel, as they engage in similar labours.

Messengers may be called swift, from the rapidity and ease with which they are conveyed. In this view, it may have respect to the naval vessels which distinguish their country, and are so well adapted, for aiding them in every part of their destined employment.

The central and eastern regions of Asia, are generally supposed to be the present seats of the Israelitish dispersion. What nation, then, of Christendom can convey with so much ease and expedition, as the American, their messengers, to the shores of that vast and unexplored country? What nation is better qualified to search and to discover them, in their unknown retreats?

Sheltered in the capacious bosom of mountains that reach the clouds, occupying the extensive sides of rivers, rapid and broad, whose waves never felt the keel, and on whose banks, a high way has never been stretched. To European missionaries, their retreat would be inaccessible without great expense of time and labour. Those obstacles oppose difficulties easily surmounted by the nation of the Canoe. Bred with the paddle in their hand, and taught to construct vessels lighter than the bulrush, they can ascend every stream, wind round the feet of every mountain, and, as circumstances require, they can either carry their canoes, or may be carried in them.

Fathers of piety and zeal, rouse your exertions! Sons that burn with holy ambition to enter into the service of the captain of your salvation, prepare with loins girded, and lamps well trimmed, for receiving the call of your Lord!

The description of the people to whom the messengers are sent, next claim our attention. Of all the nations that dwell on earth their degradation and distress appear the greatest, and yet they are represented as the peculiar objects of divine solicitude. Their name, as unnecessary, is not mentioned; for no person acquainted with the scriptures and with the history of the Jews, will hesitate to apply the description, to that unhappy people.

To a nation dispersed.] This part of the description is peculiarly their own and has no parallel in history. Nations have been found in slavery and oppression: nations have been dispersed among other nations and have lost their original name: nations have been incorporated with other nations without injury or dishonour; but the Jewish nation alone has been dispersed and still exist, a distinct people without any perceptible change of national character, in manners, government or religion.

This is the accomplishment of a prediction coeval with the existence of the nation; " And the Lord shall scatter thee among " all nations from one end of the earth to the other, and thou shalt " find no ease, nor shall the sole of thy foot find rest.", Deuteronomy, xxviii. 64, 65.

No nation has been permitted to refuse them a residence: no nation, either by persuasion or by threats, has been able to withdraw them from their national and religious habits: no nation, with all their hatred and resentments, has been allowed to extirpate or to enslave them. Scattered, killed and not destroyed!

Jews may be found in every climate, from the burning line to the frozen pole, under every government, free and despotic, among persons of every religious denomination—Hindoo, Moslem, Christian, without suffering the least change of national character.

Physiologists describe an animal of a singular nature, which when cut in pieces, every section becomes a complete polypus, perfect in every respect as the original body. The Jew is a polypus in the moral world. Divided and subdivided, united or separated, this nation appears in every section, in every assemblage completely Jewish.

This stability of disposition, formed no part of their original character. Never was there a people, previous to this prophecy, more fickle, or more prone to imitate the manners of their neighbours, and to adopt their government and religion. No remonstrance, no correction, could restrain or reclaim them. Fickleness produced their corruption, their ruin, their dispersion. God has now enstamped on them a new character. It is designed as a sign, that he intends to collect and reconcile them again without schism into one national body under Messiah their head. Dispersed Israelites, hear, and in full confidence obey the call of your own prophet. " Come and let us return to the Lord, for he " hath torn and he will heal us, he hath smitten and he will bind us " up : after two days he will revive us, on the third he will raise " us up, and we shall live in his sight." Hosea, vi. 1, 2.

And plundered.] This describes the oppression and injustice to which this people are exposed in their property. The word seems selected to intimate the cruelty that accompanies the depredation. Peeled, as those who have their hair and garments, their ornament and covering wantonly plucked off, to gratify the malignity as well as the cupidity of their spoilers. This has been awfully and universally realized.

For many years they have been ignobly industrious and remarkably inoffensive and submissive. Far from screening them from injury and injustice; this seems to have invited both. Every nation in Europe, in Asia, and Africa has stained their character and their history, with the pillage of the Jews.

Among innumerable instances on record we shall only refer to a flagrant example recorded by Hume, in his history of England, vol. 2. chap. 10.

Jewish societies wherever dispersed may be aptly compared to hives of Bees. Separated from all the world besides, with incessant labour and application and from sources neglected by others, they gather their scanty stores in which they highly delight. No sooner have they laid up sufficient to gladden their own hearts and to attract the notice of their foes, than their treasure is rudely seized by some merciless plunderer. Nor is it unfrequent, that with their hard earned wealth, they also lose their lives. None endure losses of this nature with more grief and regret; but they are never discouraged. Instantly, as if destined by heaven to provide for others, they renew their toils on the same spot, and among the same ravagers, with the cheerless prospect, that whenever their acquisitions shall invite temptation, the same calamity shall be repeated.

This is the exclusive inheritance of the Jew. Two thousand years have nearly elapsed since in every nation under heaven they have endured these indignities. Who can read this and continue to doubt the authenticity of the scriptures? Oh that the eye of these prodigal children would catch these lines, consider the cause of their suffering, and return under the guidance of their own Messiah, where, in their Fathers house they would enjoy great kindness and ample protection!

A people of terror, even in the extreme.] Our English translation neither corresponds with the Hebrew, nor with the scope of the passage, nor with the history of the people described. The word in the original is in the passive voice and represents the people as subjects of terror and not as the authors of dread to others. The design of the whole description is to mark the Jews as in the most abject, forlorn and contemptible condition.

The Jews from the call of Abraham to this hour never appeared terrible to any nation. They were considered by the nations, as Isaac by Ishmael, objects of ridicule and contempt. Nor is their conduct and courage, after the crucifixion of Christ, an exception. Their desperate deeds, and contempt of death rendered them objects of horror, rather than of terror to the Romans. On every occasion they discovered more of the desperation, the despair of the coward, than the courage of the collected and brave. Conscious of their own cruel and faithless hearts they dared not to rely on the humanity, the generosity, the promises of the Romans. In no instance, and at no time were their terror, their cowardice, and fears more conspicuous, than when in wild despair they became their own executioners after imbruing their hands in the blood of their friends, their wives and their children.

This terror Moses predicted. "If ye shall despise my statutes, I will even appoint over you terror, and the Lord shall give you a trembling heart and failing of eyes, and horror of mind, and thy life shall hang in doubt before thee, and thou shalt fear day and night and shall have none assurance of life." Levit. xxvi. 16—Deut. xxviii. 65, 66.

Ever since the day, that this nation marred the visage of the son of God, the mark of Cain has been branded deep, on their brow, and his terrors dwell in their heart; nor have dread and suspicion ever departed from their dwellings. No Jew however personally innocent and amiable he may be, but discovers to every discerning eye timidity and restlessness. Europeans observe this mark. Travellers inform us that among Hindoos and Turks it escapes not their notice. Terror, more than persecution, have urged them to seek concealment in the deep recesses of Asia. Buchanan's Christian Researches, pages 218—219. Boston edition.

In the very extreme.] On comparing, with other passages of scripture, this phrase of many translations, this appears to be the most obvious meaning. Perhaps without charge of extravagance, some might read, *from that event, even to the present time.* From the death of Christ the principal cause of their sorrows, till the period of their restoration, the Jews shall continue a nation devoted to terror. This would amount to nearly the same as our translation.

A nation of expectation, of expectation.] This is a well known form of speech among the Hebrews, employed to express great, intense, unremitting expectation. To the Jews this epithet may be applied with the utmost propriety, but to no other people on earth.

This expectation began with Abraham, the founder of the nation. He was the son of " hope," and rejoiced with gladness in the expectation of Messiah's reign. " Many prophets and righteous men died with a strong desire of seeing this period " Paul declared before Agrippa: " I am judged for the hope of the " promise made of God unto the Fathers, unto which promise " our twelve tribes, instantly serving God day and night hope to " come." Acts xxvi. 6, 7.

Ever since the destruction of Jerusalem the expectation of the Jews, wherever scattered, is as strong as in the days of John the Baptist. This expectation, has exposed them to great impositions from false Christs, and involved them in dreadful calamities and disgrace. But nothing can extinguish their hope. The expectation at this hour is as strong as ever, and is cherished wherever a Jew is found.

Buchanan, a British Missionary, in the year 1803, visited different Jewish settlements in India, and reports: " In many interesting conferences with them, two things struck me forcibly. Their constant reference to the DESOLATION of Jerusalem, and their confident hope that it shall be REBUILT. Their hope of

" rebuilding the walls of Jerusalem, the third time under the
" auspices of Messiah, is always expressed with great confi-
" dence. They have a general impression that their deliverance
" is not very remote. They say it is a sure sign of our approach-
" ing restoration, that in almost all countries there is a GENERAL
" RELAXATION of the persecution against us."

De Chateaubriand's reflections on Jerusalem and the Jews, (1806,) are pertinent and beautiful.

" What they did five thousand years ago they still continue to
" do. Seventeen times have they witnessed the destruction of
" Jerusalem, yet nothing can discourage them, nothing can pre-
" vent them from turning their faces to Zion. To see the Jews
" scattered over the whole world according to the word of God
" must doubtless excite surprize, but to be struck with super-
" natural astonishment, you must view them at Jerusalem, you
" must behold these rightful masters of Judea, living as slaves
" and strangers in their own country, you must behold them un-
" der all apprehensions *expecting* a king who is to deliver them.
" Crushed by the cross that condemns them and is planted on
" their heads, skulking near the temple, of which not one stone
" is left upon another, they continue in their deplorable infatua-
" tion. The Persians, the Greeks and the Romans are swept from
" the earth, and a petty tribe whose origin preceded that of those
" great nations, still exists, among the ruins of its native land.
" If any thing among nations wears the character of a miracle,
" that character in my opinion is here legibly impressed." *Cha-
tecubriand's Travels,* p. 407. Phila. edition.

Trodden down.] This respects the personal outrages to which this nation and people are exposed. This part of the description applies to the Jews with evidence irresistible. The cruelties of every kind which they have endured, exceed in duration and degree, not only that of any one nation, but of all the nations of the earth, besides. They have literally been trodden down, like grapes in the wine vat, with expressions of joy instead of grief.

The Romans who boasted that their ruling passion was to crush the proud and to, " spare the submissive," forgetting in the destruction of Jerusalem, every sentiment of pride and humanity, exercised the most savage cruelty and rage on the miserable remains of that infatuated nation. Regardless of age, of sex and of dignity, they trode down those who resisted, and those who sued for mercy, as reptiles the most vile and noxious.

On the shores of the sea of Galilee the same wanton outrage was renewed. Offenders and not offending, because Jews, were equally involved in destruction. The bodies of those who fell were left unburied, till the air infected, destroyed their destroyers. The transparent waters of the lake, were empurpled with blood, and covered with the floating dead. Jordan, that once opened a passage for this nation into their own country, had his own passage impeded by the carcases of her miserable children, slain by the enemy on her own plains. Twelve hundred prisoners who implored mercy, were marched to Tiberias and literally trodden to death in the amphitheatre. The most humane Emperors that ever wore the imperial purple, were spectators—were instigators! The judgment was from heaven! They were the executioners.

The streets of every nation in Europe have witnessed scenes of Jewish carnage. Their deaths have been attended with the joy of those who tread the vintage, rather than with the grief of those, who were sprinkled with human blood, unrighteously shed.

Even the humane Hindoo, who recoils from the blood of beast and of bird, rose with relentless fury, and with remorseless hate, engaged in Jewish massacre. The city of *Cranganor*, displayed scenes of blood hardly less attrocious in cruelty and extent than those of Jerusalem and Galilee. See Buchanan, p. 219, 220. Boston edition.

Ever since this unhappy nation, estimated the life of their Messiah, the desire of nations, at thirty pieces of silver, the price of a dog, they receive the opprobrious name of *Jewish Dogs* from every nation on earth, and endure the indignities offered to that impure animal.

In many of the countries in the east, Jews are not permitted to live in the same parts of the city with other inhabitants: they are excluded from every honourable office: they are compelled to perform the most degrading work and to toil in arts the least respectable. In the capital of Yemen they are not allowed to dwell nor to lodge within the walls of the city. *See Niebuhr's Travels passim.*

Infidels of talents, and education, seriously compare these facts with the prediction, and unless determined to abandon reason and modesty, dare not insinuate that the scriptures are either cunningly or foolishly devised fables!

Descendants of Abraham, formerly so highly honoured of God reflect on your present afflicted condition and the causes of it. Listen to the prediction of your own favourite prophet, and turn not away your eyes any longer from the man of sorrows, whom your Father's in ignorance and unbelief crucified. He still regards you with compassion and with love. Embrace him as the glory of Israel and soon will you hear : " Arise, shine, for thy light " is come, and the glory of the Lord is risen upon thee."

Rise, American ambassadors, and prepare to carry the tidings of joy and salvation, to your Saviour's kinsmen in disgrace—so deep and of so long duration!

A people whose country the rivers have spoiled.] This step completes the climax. The land is exposed to grief and disgrace corresponding to those of its owners. Expelled more than seventeen hundred years, scattered to the extremities of the world, destitute of any sure dwelling place, God has not extinguished their claim and title, to the inheritance of Jacob, the glory of all lands. It bears their name, it remains unclaimed by any, all who know it acknowledge, that it is the land of the Jews. But how greatly changed in beauty and riches, from that country which Moses describes ; " a good land, a land of brooks of water, " of fountains and depths that spring out of vallies and hills, a " land of wheat and barley, and vines and fig-trees, and pome- " granates ; a land of oil, olive and honey ; a land, wherein thou " shalt eat bread without scarceness, thou shalt not lack any thing " in it ; a land whose stones are iron, and out of whose hills thou " mayest dig much brass." Deut. viii. 7, 8, 9.

O! Jerusalem, O! Palestina, the rivers have spoiled thee! Thy flocks and thy herds are all swept away! Thy cities and villages sunk in earth, cannot be traced! Thy vineyards and thine olive-yards uprooted, are borne away! Land of honey, thy bees have forsaken thy rocks! The very soil of thy hills and of thy vallies has been torn up with the inundation and has disappeared! A bloody Arab, a polluted Moslem brandishes the scymetar where David once swayed the sceptre! The songs of vintage, of new moons, of Zion is heard no more ! Thou sittest in dust as a widow forsaken, and bereft of all her children !

Rivers, is a prophetic metaphor employed in describing hostile nations rushing like floods, into fertile and cultivated countries, and spreading destruction and desolation over the whole. No country on earth hath suffered ravages of this kind more numerous and destructive than Judea since the time of this prediction. The Assyrian ; the Chaldean ; the Syrian and Egyptian, successors of Alexander ; the Romans ; the Saracens ; the Crusaders ; and the Turks, have followed in succession—They poured in their forces like rivers, not for settlement, but for devastation. They have literally spoiled the land.

The accurate and affecting account which *Doctor Edward D. Clarke*, has recently given of this country furnishes an exact and extensive commentary on this part of the verse. *Travels in Holy Land*, chap. xiii.—xviii.

VERSE 3.

" All ye inhabitants of the world, and ye that dwell on earth,
" when the standard is lifted upon the mountains, look ye ! and
" when the trumpet is sounded, listen ye !"

NOTES AND ILLUSTRATIONS.

A new scene and a new subject are here introduced—JEHOVAH dismisses from the vision the swift messengers, and the oppressed nation. He submits to the eye of the prophet a view of the world and its various inhabitants, and with a loud voice, charges them in his hearing, to watch for his signals and to hasten to the field without delay.

By the stile and spirit of the charge, with its standard and trumpet, a battle is evidently portended. By the ardour and extent of the address, its importance to every individual of the human race is suggested. All must appear as actors—not as spectators.

From the place, in the vision, which this scene occupies, we are taught to look for this solemn summons, soon after the messengers shall have entered on their benevolent labours. Subsequent prophecies shed encreasing light on this short and pathetic prediction. Similarity of phrase and other circumstances lead us with evidence sufficiently satisfactory to refer the whole, to that decisive battle, which shall terminate the present administration of providence and grace, and prepare the world for the last and most glorious dispensation of the gospel on earth.

It is intimated in scripture that the success of the Messengers in the conversion of the Jews shall be extraordinary and rapid. " They shall run to and fro, and knowledge shall be increased." Ignorance and infidelity shall yield to the powerful influence of the gospel. New born desires and united endeavours shall be produced of returning to their own land and of submitting themselves to Jesus their king. They shall commence their journey powerfully aided by the very nations that formerly despised and oppressed them.

The report of their advance, their numbers and their pious zeal, shall reach and alarm the churches of Antichrist. Alliances with infidel nations shall be formed, and they shall undertake an expedition with numerous forces to oppose the return and re-settlement of the converted Jews in Judea. Their collected forces shall assemble near the eastern shores of the Mediterranean, at the ancient Megiddo, which from the destruction that shall follow, shall be known, for ever after with the addition of *charem*, *a curse*, by the name of Armageddon.

The place of mustering, and the delusive arts that shall be employed, to engage the nations and their kings in this fatal war, are beautifully described by John the Divine : " And I saw three un-
" clean spirits, like frogs, come out of the mouth of the Dragon,
" and out of the mouth of the Beast, and out of the mouth of the
" False Prophet, for they are the spirits of Devils working mira-
" cles, which go forth unto the kings of the earth and of the
" whole world, to gather them to the battle of the great day of
" God almighty, and he gathered them together into a place call-
" ed in the Hebrew tongue Armageddon." Rev. xvi. 13, 14, 16.

From Armageddon this vast and mixed army shall ascend the mountains of Judea, according to the prophecy of Daniel. " He
" shall plant the tabernacles of his palaces between the seas in
" the glorious holy mountain." Daniel xi. 45.

On these mountains also JEHOVAH shall lift up his ensign, which shall be seen by all the inhabitants of the world. Probably he shall display some splendid meteor like the star which guided the wise men of the east to the cradle of the new-born Redeemer.

Its influence on every eye and on every heart shall be irresistible, but various. It shall fill the hearts of those who know and receive it as the Banner of their Lord with joy inexpressible, and they shall hasten to witness the victory of the captain of their salvation. By them the prediction in the text, shall then be understood. But this ensign shall fill the army of the enemies of Christ with rage and fury; and perhaps impelled by those impure spirits which delude them, it may be employed, to lure them in confidence of victory, to their defeat and destruction.

The trumpet shall sound, and at its blast the armies and their leaders shall prepare for the combat. "The feet of Jehovah "shall stand in that day on the mount of Olives, which is before "Jerusalem on the east." He shall cry "assemble yourselves "and come all ye heathen and gather yourselves together round "about. Thither cause thy mighty ones to come down O Lord." Zach. xiv. 4, 5. Joel iii. 4, 12. How little shall the heathen think that God gives the word of command!

Let us now attend to this scene as described by John, Rev. xix. 11.—19.

" I saw Heaven opened, and behold a white horse, and he that "sat on him was called faithful and true, and in righteousness "doth he judge and make war. His eyes were like a flame of fire "and on his head were many crowns: and he had a name written 'that no man knew but himself, and he was clothed with a vesture dipped in blood and his name is called THE WORD OF GOD, "and the armies which were in heaven followed him upon white "horses clothed in fine linen, white and clean, and out of his "mouth goeth a sharp two edged sword, that with it he should "smite the nations, and he shall rule them with a rod of iron." Against them shall the opposing host advance. And "I saw the "beast and the kings of the earth and their armies gathered "together to make war against him that sat on the horse and "against his army."

The issue of the battle, on the part of the saints and their king shall be decisive and glorious. The sword which he shall employ is the word of his mouth, by which he shall command the artillery of heaven to descend, and in a moment shall fearfully destroy his enemy, and that, *without hands*. His followers shall have only to witness the strength of his glorious arm, that secures to him the victory, and to raise in gratitude and admiration the song of

triumph. Of the victory, John writes: " And the beast was
" taken, and with him the false prophet that wrought miracles
" before him, with which he deceived them that had received the
" mark of the beast, and them that worshipped his image. These
" both were cast alive into a lake of fire burning with brimstone,
" and the remnant were slain with the sword of him that sat
" upon the horse which proceeds out of his mouth." Rev. xix.
20, 21.

The time when this battle shall take place, though predicted
with remarkable precision, both by the prophet Daniel and the
evangelist John, has greatly perplexed and divided the conjectures
of christian interpreters. God it appears has fixed the period,
and for wise reasons left the year in obscurity till revealed by the
event.

In several prophecies, two singular sovereign powers, one in
the west and the other in the east, both hostile to the christian
cause, are represented as rising within the pale of christianity.
Their reign is limited to 1260 years. At the expiration of these
years the battle shall take place and terminate their reign, and
existence. It is generally supposed, and supported by powerful
arguments, that the Papal and Mahometan governments so diverse in their nature and progress from all others, hitherto
known, are the powers predicted.

In the year of our Lord, 606, the Papal power made its first
appearance in Rome, and the Mahometan in the very same year in
Medina. If we admit this as the real commencement of the 1260
years, we may expect the battle in 1866. But it may be alledged
that though they rose and received their *right* to their sovereign-
ties in that year, they did not actually *exercise* it, nor were pub-
licly *recognized*, till some years afterwards. For the years of sove-
reigns are numbered not from their birth, but from the time of
their investiture and entering on the execution of their office.
This will make the time of the battle so much later than 1866 as
their legal entering on office shall be posterior to the time when
they receive their right. Perhaps, as in the case of the seventy
years captivity, the prophecy may have a double accomplishment.

About the year 1866, we may expect, if not the battle, some
important event. The swift messengers must receive the call,
some years at least before the battle, for the converts shall constitute a part of the army that shall follow the Messiah. Angels of

the American churches rise and make ready! It appears that you are on the very eve of receiving the call. Continue like the waiting apostles in prayer and preparation till your Lord visit you according to his promise!

Verse 4.

" Then, thus did JEHOVAH say to me, I will now sit still, and I
" will now look intently from my habitation, like serene heat after
" clear sunshine, and like a dewy cloud in the heat of harvest."

NOTES AND ILLUSTRATIONS.

Then, thus did JEHOVAH *say to me.*] This verse presents a new subject delivered in a new mode of revelation. The contents of the three first verses were submitted to the eye of the prophet and accompanied with explanation by the voice of God. They were fitted for vision as peculiarly affecting and pathetic. The subject of this verse is more abstruse and mysterious and less suited to the public ear; it is therefore spoken in confidence to the prophet himself.

The intention of JEHOVAH it appears, is to announce the plan on which he had determined to conduct the government of the world from that time till the battle of Armageddon. Hitherto his agency, in the direction and controul of human affairs, had been obviously remarkable. His voice and his arm had openly associated temporal blessings and temporal judgments with distinguished piety, and with atrocious crimes. The deluge, the overthrow of Sodom, the defeat and destruction of Pharoah, of Midian and of Senacherib, revealed the immediate hand of the avenger and judge. The protection of Abraham and of Joseph, of David and of Hezekiah, proclaimed him the guide and defender of innocence and piety oppressed. His whole administration respecting the tribes of Jacob, from their admission into the land of Palestine, till the time of this prophecy exhibited God, in constant action, as their guide, their protector and their judge.

The time had now arrived, destined by the wisdom of Heaven, when he was to withdraw himself more from human eye, and to conceal his agency, in the temporal affairs of men. His wonderful deeds had been committed to imperishable records, and by tradition had been spread among the nations of the earth. Predictions had now extended the view of the church not only to the days of the Son of man, but to the end of time. The person, the character, the doctrines, the life and the death of th Messiah, had been delineated with such accuracy, and in such extent, that the evangelists and apostles, have added little else to them, than the historical form.

The vineyard thus prepared, the husbandman shall withdraw his personal presence from it, and while secretly dispensing his influence, shall remain in his habitation waiting till the time of vintage.

I will now sit still.] The word, *now*, is introduced as expressive of the emphatic letter added, to the verb in the original. To sit still, is a scripture phrase, applied to God when he retires from conspicuous labour, or seems to delay the execution of his judgments. On the evening of the sixth day when the external works of creation were completed, God is said to enter into his rest. The Psalmist, in his distress, frequently calls on him, to rise and scatter his enemies.

God had now prepared like a vineyard, the system of his moral government, and was about to withdraw his voice and his arm from the view of the world. His agency, though continued, was seldom to appear, except thro' the laws that he had established in his word, and in his works. He was, like the husbandman, to retire from the public eye, into his tower, from which he might inspect and order unseen the affairs of his vineyard, and thus wait till the time of vintage.

About the end of the Jewish captivity, this change in his administration took place, and still continues. The ladder which reached from heaven to earth, and on which angels had for ages, descended and ascended from God to men, was removed. The spirit of prophecy, which had continued to instruct the church, in a succession of inspired teachers, disappeared. The oracle, which since the days of Moses, furnished divine counsel, in critical emergencies, became silent.

The visits of that God, whose presence shook the mountains and divided the waves, were repeated no more. No more, was his holy arm made bare, to humble the rebellious proud, and to save the oppressed of the earth.

Infliction of awful judgments, on the criminal and impious was restrained. Jerusalem and Rome might surpass Sodom and

Babylon in cruelty and wickedness, without suffering everlasting destruction, by inundation and flame.

Ahabs and Jezabels, have risen and tormented the Jewish and the christian church, and have been permitted to prolong their lives in honour, and to descend into the tombs of their Fathers without tasting the signal vengeance of insulted heaven. How many despisers of divine institutions, have escaped the leprosy of Miriam, and the dreadful descent into hell alive, with Korah and his rebellious associates? How many priests have offered strange fire, on gospel altars, without being consumed at their feet, like Nadab and Abihu? The Nero's, the Herods, with the French, the Roman and the British persecutors, have drank the blood of the saints, and have not lost their first born, and their own lives like Pharoah in the execution of their bloody deeds. Nay, at the time when Jew and Gentile, when priests and magistrates, accused, insulted, afflicted, condemned and crucified his only begotten Son, God appeared to sit still, though the rocks sympathized with the sufferer, and the sun and earth testified their horror, at the heaven daring deed! The language of providence was in the words of the Saviour: " Let them grow together till the harvest."

Sons of violence, of prosperity and of irreligion, your present peace arises from the dispensation, and not from the approbation of God! He sits still, but he looks intently from his holy habitation.

Meek and faithful sufferers of the lamb, follow him with patience; there is a *need be*, for your present sorrows, that ye may reign with him in glory.

" God shall come and shall not keep silence—A fire shall devour
" before him, and it shall be very tempestuous round about him.
" He shall call to the heaven and to the earth. Gather my saints
" together unto me."

I will now look intently from my habitation.] This feature of his administration denotes his constant attention to his vineyard. Though silent and unseen; " He looketh from the heavens, he
" beholdeth all the sons of men. From the place of his habita-
" tion, he looketh upon all the inhabitants of the earth. He con-
" sidereth all their works." Psal. xxxiii. 13, 14, 15.

Of the nature of this inspection, Christ himself gives specimens. " He that holdeth the seven stars in his right hand, saith,

" I know thy works, and thy labours, and thy patience and how
" thou canst not bear them that are evil, and for my names sake
" hast laboured, and not fainted. I know thy works, and tribula-
" tion, and poverty; but thou art rich. I know where thou dwel-
" lest, even where Satan's seat is. Be faithful unto the death."

" He that hath the sharp sword with two edges, saith:—I know
" that thou hast a name, that thou livest and art dead, I know
" that thou art neither cold, nor hot, but luke-warm, I will spue
" thee out of my mouth. Thou sayest, I am rich, and increas-
" ed with goods, and have need of nothing, and knowest not, that
" thou art wretched and miserable, and poor, and blind, and naked.
" Repent, or else I will fight against thee with the sword of my
" mouth." Revelation ii. iii.

The eye of God sees the conduct and searches the heart. He records every action and will bring every secret thing into judgment. Though silent; his detestation of sin, is as strong as if he reproved in tempest and thunder. The service, the tears, and the pious trust, of those who fear him, are beheld with as much complacency as if an angel should announce; " thy prayers and " thine alms come up for a memorial before God."

Bright sun shine.] This appears sufficiently literal and well adapted to the design of the text. The common version, is *herbs*. Horsley translates it *lightening*, and Lowth, *grass*. Neither of them offer satisfactory reasons, in support of their versions. Lowth, with infantile candour, adds, " This meaning of the word " seems to make the best sense in this place; it were to be wish-
" ed that it were better supported."

The word occurs first, in the opening of the book of Genesis, God said let there be *light* and there was *light*. In every place where we afterwards meet with it, Job. xxxvii. 11. not excepted, it preserves the same signification.

Bright *sun* shine, is indispensably necessary for the production of the grape. Vines demand the sunny hill. They must be planted in such order, that every plant may receive without obstruction, the genial rays of the sun. Without his potent beam the bud is never happily protruded, nor the blossom successfully unfolded. The word *light*, which by circumlocution, we translate *bright sun shine*, evidently is designed, to mark this effect. Till the bud and blossom are evolved, the serene heat can be of no avail.

Light, in scripture, and especially in the gospel by John, is synonimous with life. " In him was life and the life was the light " of men." In the context Christ is declared the creator of the material world. Here he is represented as the author of the vital, spiritual principle. If we could safely consider the expression as including vegetable and animal, as well as moral life, we might view *light* in this place as the vegetable principle. This would equally suit the metaphorical application of the phrase.

Like serene heat.] This is necessary to cherish and protect the bursting bud and the expanding blossom. Cold at that period would chill; and the rude blast would scatter the tender embrio's in the destructive storm. A judge on this subject exclaims:

"Eheu, quid volui misero mihi? floribus Austrum,
"Perditus——immisi."—— *Virg. Eclog:* ii. 59.

The metaphor in the text, reveals that gracious and mild government, about to be established, and under which we now live. " God is causing his sun to shine and his rain to descend equally " on the evil and on the good." The labours and the exertions of the wicked, shall share in this serene heat and terminate with as much success, as those of the just. Impiety and injustice, under this mild dispensation, neither dread nor suffer temporal judgments. Profligacy and intemperance are supplied, with abundance, without feeling the rebuke and scourge of him, whose goodness they abuse. Honour and prosperity, dwell in the tabernacles of monsters, the destroyers of human happiness, who deluge the world with blood, and force the tears from those, of whom the world is not worthy.

God is furnishing every thing necessary for securing a generous vintage, while they are abusing them to his dishonour and their own ruin. " He leaves not himself without a witness in granting " them fruitful seasons, filling their hearts with food and glad- " ness."

It is true, that fearful and frequent calamities, take place under this dispensation. But these are not judgments inflicted from heaven; but the fruits which wickedness, by the eternal laws of wisdom produces. They form no part of that punishment which God as a righteous judge, reserves for the wicked. They resemble the pains and remorse of the criminal, and not the stroke of the executioner.

ISAIAH, CHAP XVIII. V. 4.

Singular piety, under this *still conducted* administration receives no peculiar external protection or reward. Her privileges belong to another kingdom invisible to the world, and disregarded by it. Her afflictions arise either from herself or from surrounding circumstances, from which God never intended nor promised that she should receive *serene heat*. Such afflictions when patiently borne shall however ripen her " for a far more exceeding and eternal weight of glory."

Like a dewy cloud in the heat of harvest.] Harvest is a critical season to the vines. The heat, which the productions of the field require, to enrich, and mature them, would prove destructive to the vineyard. To mitigate the intemperate heat of this season providence raises an easy and seasonable remedy. In harvest when the days are intolerably arid, the nights lengthen and become chilling. This change of atmosphere generates copious dews in the vallies which surround the hilly vineyards. With the rising sun these dews ascend in fleecy clouds and veil the vineyard, refresh the grape, and oppose a transparent covering to the autumnal sun.

God in the text engages to provide *dewy clouds* of a moral texture, in the same secret and mysterious manner, for the shelter of the plants of his moral vineyard. As his natural dews fall alike on grapes of every quality, so shall his moral dews on his moral plants. This is a subject delicate and difficult. It distinguishes the present plan of providence. It extends alike to nations and to individuals, to objects the most magnificent and the most minute.

In how many instances, since the prediction has been uttered, have destroying tyrants risen, followed by infatuated nations and have threatened not only the peace, but the existence of the race of man. Intoxicated by success, exasperated by opposition, and hardened to human sensibility, by cruel deeds, they would have made the world a complete desolation, had not God interposed. His invisible hand spread the toils in which they have been intangled and raised the apparently contemptible object that said, " thou shalt proceed no farther." Europe has recently furnished, and continues to furnish illustrations of this subject that awaken the attention of the most torpid, and compel infidelity herself to own that there is a God who now works silently but most powerfully.

The politic and powerful attempts to establish universal monarchy, on the ruins of the Roman empire, on which God had prophesied, that ten kingdoms shall stand till the day of the battle shall come ;—have all been crushed by an agency unseen.

The attempts of christendom, to extirpate the disciples of Mahomet before the period of their vintage, have all proved abortive. Infidel France, with her associates, could only wound without destroying the papal power, because her grapes are not yet ripe.

Ten successive persecutions, within the space of a few years, after the commencement of christianity, threatened to extinguish the christian name. How vain their efforts? He, who looks from his habitation, with his dewy cloud defeated the attempts. Errors rose supported by eloquence and defended by power that appeared to undermine the foundations of the church. In *Athanasius* and *Cyprian* ; in *Augustine* and *Luther*, appear the dewy clouds, that cherished and defended the planting of the Lord's right hand.

Particular critical periods, in the lives of Charles V. and his bigotted and cruel son Philip; of Henry VIII. of England, and of the house of Guise in France, furnish materials, in abundance to show the secret, but powerful agency of God in his vineyard.

In humble life, in domestic scenes, in individual adventure, evidences of the same agency multiply. Let the proud and arrogant Pharisee, who boasts in his morality, listen and he may hear the whisper—*I kept thee back*. Observe the real christian, and on every deliverance, and at the close of every successful exertion, you will find him inscribing on his grateful memory, *Ebenezer*.

Enter into the cabin of poverty, and profligacy in the purlieus of populous cities, even there you must read a comment on the text. Mark that wretch with quivering lip, pouring out blasphemy and murder! view him convulsed by disappointment, by remonstrance, by inebriation and remorse! Watch his wildly rolling eye balls, and his hand grasping the instrument of death! The night advances,—in darkness, his wife and innocent babes, whom he had once sworn to protect, standing in tears and terror, without strength or protector.... What are your anticipations of the morning scene.... Mangled corpses before the frantic murderer! No! All is serene and smiling, and the storm forgotten! What could produce a scene so unexpected? *The dewy cloud of your God.* They were not yet ripe for misery or for mercy. The picture is not over charged. Such terrific scenes are often reacted. The result the same—God reigns.

Verse 5.

" But while the harvest was passing away, when the bud had
" become perfect, and the blossom had changed into the juicy
" grape: He cut down the luxuriant branches with pruning hooks!
" he removed the standard vine! he cut in pieces!"

NOTES AND ILLUSTRATIONS.

This is a new subject, forming a part of the general vision and intimately connected with the preceding verse. The relation stops, and the vineyard itself rises in scenic representation, to the prophet's eye. From the description he must have instantly recognized the vineyard. Jehovah is therefore silent, and Isaiah under apparent agitation of mind, reports what he saw.

While the harvest was passing away.] Harvest in the original appears personified. It is represented in the attitude of preparation, ready to surrender all the fruits of its season, in full perfection to vintage approaching, and ready to receive them with joy. This personification, unnoticed, has been the chief source of ambiguity in almost every translation. It is generally translated *before harvest*. This though *verbal*, is not just. It intimates that the scene took place before the time of harvest, while it is evident from what follows that it was at the very close of it. The obscurity will be removed, if we translate literally, *in the presence of*, or, *under the eye of harvest*. Harvest had not yet retired, nor had vintage actually entered the vineyard. At this interesting period, The calamity, The awful summons, The dreadful conflict will probably happen when the prospects of the devoted victims have become most flattering: This is often the case, at the fall and death of the prosperous wicked.

When the bud had become perfect.] This is the first important change in the vine. The sun had acted with full influence, and had given a favourable birth to the bud. The *serene* heat had in due season, succeeded to the powerful sunbeam. The blossom had spread itself in all its beauty and fragrance. The destroying touch of cold and frost had not been felt. The agitating storm had not shaken off one of its delicate leaves. The embrio grape was completely formed and vigorous. All had advanced thus far to a happy vintage. Summer had fully performed her part.

The blossom had changed into the juicy grape.] This marks the second critical period in the vineyard. The embrio berry requires warmth, with moisture. Harvest often shrivels up the grape, and before, by time, it acquires its just dimension, and flavour, ripens it prematurely, and thus destroys the expectation and represses the joys of vintage. The vineyard had by the aid of the dewy cloud, escaped these dangers. The blossom had passed into the juicy mellow grape of swelling size, and generous flavour. Under such circumstances, the fears of the husbandman are all dismissed, and he prepares himself for the season of festivity. Such was the state of the vineyard which Isaiah saw. How delightful ! Such is the condition of the prosperous sinner, who retains his riches and his blushing honours till the evening of life. He views himself fortunate, and men call him happy. None deserve such titles, till the master say, come ye blessed !

He cut down the luxuriant branches with pruning hooks.] We may suppose that the prophet waited for the arrival of the husbandman, accompanied with grape gatherers, bearing their baskets with all the expressions of joy usual on such occasions, and with the vintage song. On a sudden Jehovah, in whose presence he stood, advanced with his ponderous pruning hook, and probably, as hooks are in the plural, with all his angels with him. No countenance of joy, no song. The countenance of disappointment and vengeance prevailed. A pruning hook in a vineyard at the opening of vintage, is an instrument out of season.

With this instrument, instead of the *barren*, he cut down the most *luxuriant* branches, regardless of their rich clusters, and lays them inglorious on the ground. Fruit and branch, the glory of the present year, and the hope of the following are completely destroyed ! The name of the person, so conspicuous, in his terror, he mentions not. Nor was it necessary. Who but Jehovah, the master of the vineyard, could perform this dreadful work!

We translate the verb in the past tense. The conjunctive particle, is rather emphatic than conversive. The scope of the passage, the great arbiter of tenses in the Hebrew language, demands this tense. A vision always implies the real existence of what is seen, and requires the translation in the perfect or present tenses. Predictions, for the same reason as they represent what is not in existence, always demand the future. Fuller observations, on *particular grammar* will not be necessary to oriental scholars, and can not be well understood by others.

He removed the standard vine.] This appears to be the translation of the phrase. It is designed to represent complete destruction of the vineyard. Nor root, nor branch of these degenerate plants, shall ever after encumber, and pollute the ground. He cast them out of the vineyard.

He cut in pieces.] This expresses the marks of his displeasure, and of his vengeance, even when cast out of the vineyard. Death shall not terminate the disgrace and punishment of sinners. They shall be delivered to the tormentors. As he cuts, he will add, "Let no fruit grow on thee hereafter, for ever."

This scene, and this work is affecting, if confined to a common vineyard, they would mark great provocation and disappointment. But it rises in importance, when we know that it is emblematical of the dreadful destruction of sinners in the battle of Armageddon. Omitting other passages of scripture, and arguments on a point in which few differ, we only produce the following: " Beat
" your plowshares into swords, and your pruning hooks into
" spears. Put ye in the sickle, for the harvest is ripe. Come
" get you down, for the press is full, the vats over flow, for their
" wickedness is great." Joel iii. 10, 13.

" And I looked and beheld, a white cloud, and upon the cloud
" sat one like the son of man, having on his head, a golden crown,
" and in his hand a sharp sickle, and another angel came out of
" the temple, crying, with a loud voice, to him that sat on the
" cloud: Thrust in thy sickle, and reap: For the harvest of the
" earth is ripe. And he that sat on the throne, thrust in his sickle
" on the earth: and the earth was reaped. And another angel
" came out, from the altar, which had power over fire: and cried

"with a loud voice to him that had the sharp sickle, saying, thrust
"in thy sharp sickle, and gather the clusters of the vine of the
"earth: for her grapes are fully ripe. And the angel thrust in
"his sickle into the earth and gathered the vine of the earth, and
"cast it into the great wine-press of the wrath of God. And the
"wine-press was trodden without the city, and blood came out of
"the wine-press, unto the horse' bridles, by the space of a thou-
"sand and six hundred furlongs." Rev. xv. 14, 20.

The agent, in this dread scene is described by Isaiah: "Who
"is this that cometh from Edom with dyed garments from
"Bozrah? This that is glorious in his apparel travelling in the
"greatness of his strength! I that speak in righteousness
"mighty to save. Wherefore art thou red in thine apparel, and
"thy garments like him that treadeth in the wine vat? I have trod-
"den in the wine-press alone, and of the people there was none to
"help me. For I will tread them in mine anger, and trample
"them in my fury, and their blood shall be sprinkled upon my
"garments, and I will stain all my vesture." Isa. lxiii. 1, 3.

This is the description of the great and terrible day of the
Lord. He shall then lay aside his robe of salvation, and he shall
clothe himself with vengeance like a cloak of war. The
proud of the earth can make no more resistance to him than the
grape to the pruning hook. The day of vengeance shall be in his
heart, and fearful will be the recompence of that hour.

The stroke and the agonies of death, shall be the battle of Armageddon! to every obstinate rebel, to every impenitent sinner. It
comes when every thing around smiles, and when the heart dreads
no danger. The uplifted instrument may be now taking aim, to
cut down the man whose eye passes over these lines.—Cut down,
uprooted, cast out, cut in pieces! Like the prophet, the heart pal-
pitates, the frame trembles!

Verse 6.

"They abandon them, promiscuously, to the eagle of the moun-
"tains, and to the beasts of the field. On HIM the eagle of the
"mountains is glutted, even on HIM all the beasts of the field in-
"sultingly riot."

NOTES AND ILLUSTRATIONS.

This is the last scene of this remarkable vision. The wine-press of the former verse is turned to a field of carnage, and the bruised grapes into corpses floating in their own blood.

This rapid transition from the sign to the thing signified; or from figures taken from the vegetable to those of the animal world, may at first glance appear violent and incongruous. But the description is not of scenes as they appear in nature; but as they appear in mental visions and dreams. The operations of the faculties of sensation and memory, and those of the faculty of dreaming, to which visions appear to belong, are under different laws and associations. In mental visions the principal link of association is fancied resemblance in the qualities, disposition, utility, and fitness of the subjects under review, or even of absent objects. The man and the brute, the fowl and the quadruped, the living and the dead, things near and things remote in time and in place, present resembling qualities, and the faculty of mental vision combines them and forms images the most fantastic. However absurd they may appear in our waking moments, they never offend during the operation of the faculty.

This appears to have been the case in the present instance. The colour of the juice of the vine, expressed by the indignation and disappointment of the husbandman, was easily associated by this wonderful faculty with the blood of dying men in the field of battle, under the fury and power of an offended king. Examples of the same nature occur in other scriptures, that describe the scene to which the text relates. The Saviour accounts for the colour and redness of his apparel at one time, because he had trodden the wine-press till his raiment was stained with the juice of the grape, and immediately after, he adds, that their colour was red, because he had in fury trampled on his enemies, and sprinkled all his garments with their blood, Isa. lxiii. 1, 3. The apostle John, describes this vision thus: "He gathered the vine of the "earth and cast it into the wine-press of the wrath of God, trod-"den without the city, and blood came out of the wine-press, "even to the horse' bridles." Rev. xiv. 19, 20.

The prophets saw no difficulty in these mixed representations, no incongruity. Nor shall we, if we consider it as an inspired dream, and not as a narrative addressed to the ear, or a prospect submitted to the eye.

The faculty of dreaming was no doubt originally bestowed on man for the most noble purposes. It is not improbable that it was destined, as it is still sometimes employed, for enabling us to hold converse with superior intelligences. Our apostacy from God cut off this spiritual intercourse, and renders the faculty now like an organ without its legitimate object. This may account for its vagaries; but in the wildest of them, we cannot fail to receive deep impressions of the dignity of the human soul; and the extent of its powers! Attention to this faculty in its operations and laws, as they occur occasionally in scripture, and are developed in experience is of more importance in unfolding prophetic visions and dreams recorded in scripture, than many suppose.

They abandon them.] The verb is here translated in the present tense. Every Hebrew scholar knows, that this language has no appropriate present. And strange, as it may seem to those unacquainted with the oriental languages, their future performs this office not only with sufficient precision, but with peculiar significance and force. Besides the prophet describes what he actually saw in existence; and therefore it cannot be translated in the future. Every succeeding prophet, in the old testament, and the apostle John, who wrote in Greek, in the new, where no ambiguity of tense can be even pretended, describe all their visions in the past or present time, all as having existence.

They abandon them promiscuously to the Eagle of the, &c.] The scene appears to open with the close of the engagement. The prospect fills the prophet with surprize and horror. They abandon them! On one side, the victorious army is returning in triumph. Behind them the defeated foe is left in the gory bed of death. Burial, refused by none but infuriated savages, is denied by the Prince of clemency, and his humane followers. They shrink from the touch of the bodies of miscreants detested by God and man. They account them so abominable that the house of corruption refuses to admit them. They must, dying and dead, remain exposed. The most doleful creatures of air and earth must devour, and decompose them in their bowels before they are permitted to mingle with dust. All around the heavens are blackened with flocks of birds of prey, rushing down from every mountain; and the earth trembles under the multitude and roar of savage beasts of prey, hastening from their dark retreats, to the sacrifice and feast which God had prepared, and to which he had invited them.

" Thus saith the Lord God; speak to every feathered *fowl* and " to every *beast of the field*, Assemble yourselves, and come, " gather yourselves on every side to my sacrifice, that I do sacri- " fice for you, even a great sacrifice upon the *mountains* of Israel, " that ye may eat flesh and drink blood, ye shall eat the *flesh of* " *the mighty*, and drink the *blood of the Princes* of the earth." Ezek. xxxix. 17, 18.

" And I saw an angel standing in the sun, and he cried with " a loud voice, saying to all the fowls that fly in the midst of " heaven, come, and gather yourselves together unto the supper " of the great God; that ye may *eat the flesh of kings*, and the " *flesh of captains*, and the flesh of *mighty men*." Rev. xix. 17, 18.

Who doth not see that these passages are descriptions of the scene in the text? Who can deny that they all refer to the same great day of the Lord? Who can proceed to the parts of the description omitted without observing the mixed nature of metaphors in dreams and visions and instead of receiving them with disgust, deriving peculiar pleasure from their associations.

On HIM *also shall the Eagle of the mountains, &c.*] A contrast is evidently intended between this member of the sentence and the promiscuous throng in the beginning of the verse. A character distinguished for dignity and crime; for suffering and disgrace, is here introduced. By the repetition of the pronoun, an emphasis is designed. He is not only abandoned, but exposed to the eagle, and to all the wild beasts of the field.

Let us examine the description of this battle, delivered by other prophets, and the result will at once remove every shade of obscurity from the passage, by discovering the illustrious personage, who met the Prophets eye, and held a place so conspicuous, that he thinks it unnecessary to mention his name.

Daniel says, " I beheld even till the BEAST was slain and his " body destroyed, and given to the burning flame." A double punishment is here predicted in very forcible expressions. His

F

body first destroyed, and after this destruction it was given to the flame.

John is more circumstantial. " And the BEAST was taken, and " with him the false prophet, these both were cast alive into a " lake of fire burning with brimstone." Dan. vii. 11. Rev. xix. 20, 21.

The Beast of these prophets and the nameless personage in the text, are the same. The beast, is the representative of the Roman empire, under the dominion of the dragon, attended by the Papal power or false prophet, and composed of ten kingdoms, at the time of this awful event. France, appears now, to be the representative of Rome, her chief shall probably command the rebel army, and shall be exposed to the examplary punishment and indignity described in the text. The beast and the false prophet are sometimes considered as one individual, as they were animated and directed by the same spirit, and some times as two, as they are naturally distinct, and sometimes acted in opposition.

The eagle of the mountains are glutted.] To glut, to be surfeited, to be satiated to loathing, is beyond dispute the meaning of the original. To summer upon, is a word found no where else in scripture, and rarely in the English language, never in a respectable situation, and even then with a meaning very different from what appears to be intended in the text.

The reason from etymology assigned for this translation is singular in the extreme. The word to summer it is said, is derived from the verb *to satiate*, because that season abounds with the treasures of the opening earth. Then from this derived noun, they derive a new verb, renouncing its original signification, and adopting the signification of its parent noun. But they produce no other place, nor can they produce one, where this verb conveys such meaning.

On him insultingly riot.] This appears the uniform sense of the word, wherever it occurs in scripture. But under precisely the same etymological process to which *summer on*, was submitted, it is converted *to winter on*. Further remarks would be superfluous.

This version first appears in the Vulgate Bible, revised by *Jerome*. It is probable that this excellent and stern critic, is the author both of the translation and the reasons on which it is supported. The apparently mixed metaphor offended his rules of rhetoric, and he sought relief in his etymology. His success has been such as might have been expected. Few passages of scripture can be produced in which the unwarrantable liberties of the translator is more glaring. And in attempting to render the metaphors consistent, he has been reduced to the necessity of making the eagle, the tiger, the lion, the vulture, and the wolf to feed in summer and in winter, on the branches and clusters of the vine. Had he applied to the text, the laws of visions instead of those of grammar, his trouble would have been less, and his labours more satisfactory.

In the septuagint, the most ancient version of the Scriptures, in existence, and from which the vulgate in this place borrows without benefit, the translation is thus, " upon *them* shall the " fowls of Heaven be gathered together, upon *him* shall all the " beasts of the earth come."

The spirit of the language employed breathes, punishments intolerable and of long continuance. In this respect it agrees with other scriptures on the same subject. It is not impossible that God shall preserve the bodies of the slain, from being consumed though constantly fed upon by birds and beasts, as a lasting monument of their crimes and of his wrath, and as an emblem of that everlasting torment, without annihilation, to which the wicked shall be subjected, in the eternal state. The last verse of our prophet is remarkable. " And they shall go forth and look upon " the carcases of the men that have transgressed against me : for " their worm shall not die, neither shall their fire be quenched, " and they shall be an abhorring to all flesh." See also Zach. iv. 12. Ezek. xxxix. 9—12.

By no interpretation can such passages be applied to events on record; or, to the punishments that await the wicked in a future state.

The punishment of the Beast, their king, as exceeding in wickedness and crimes, his associates, shall be correspondingly dreadful and protracted. We cannot resist the impression, made by the text, and by similar descriptions of his being exposed alive to the torments here described. John declares he was taken alive. Isaiah says, the eagle, and all the beasts, insultingly fed on him, Daniel says, his body, when destroyed, was given to the burning flame, and John affirms that he was still alive, when cast into the lake, burning with fire and brimstone. Can these texts, taken collectively lead to any other conclusion, than, that he shall actually endure tortures of body on the field of battle, till at last apparently consumed and destroyed, and yet alive, he shall like the dragon his lord, be cast into everlasting burning.

The classic reader will already have in thought recurred to the terrific fable of Tityus.

> "Incontinentis nec Titye jecur
> "Relinquit ales, nequitiæ additus,
> "Custos."—— Hor. Od. ii. 4.

This affecting portion of ancient mythology received its birth in Phenicia, and we strongly suspect with Alexander Pope, that it was stolen from the same sacred fountain from which Virgil silently and slyly drew his celebrated Pollio.

The reflections which this subject suggests, nay forces on the mind, is of the most awful and interesting nature. Our bodies may not be exposed in that field. But before that day, they may if we enlist not under the banners of the son of God, be in similar circumstances. "Except we repent we shall all likewise perish." Who can think of persisting in that course of life that shall so soon associate us with those execrable rebels? Reader, will you dare to indulge in sloth and in irresolution for another day? Will you persist in your course of crime and dissipation any longer? Will you venture for another hour to wage an impious war with heaven, by rejecting his son.—Know, "there is but a step between you and death."!

VERSE 7.

"At that time, shall a present, be brought to JEHOVAH of "hosts, of a people dispersed and pillaged; even of a people "under terror in the extreme; a nation of expectation, of expecta- "tion; and trodden down, whose country rivers have spoiled— "to the place of the name of Jehovah of hosts—Mount Zion."

NOTES AND ILLUSTRATIONS.

JEHOVAH, in his own person, introduced this remarkable prophecy and with strong emotions of pity dispatched swift American messengers to the relief of his prodigal children, in long and deep affliction. In this verse, the prophet closes the drama in strains of exultation, in view of the success, that shall crown their faithful services, in the glorious restoration of his nation.

At that time.] From the emphasis, generally allowed to the demonstrative pronoun, the text seems strongly to intimate, that the battle and oblation, shall take place on the same day. The victorious Redeemer shall hasten down from the mountains of prey, to receive with joy, "those who have turned away from "transgression in Jacob." "For then shall the redeemed of the "Lord have returned, and have come with singing unto Zion, "and with everlastng joy upon their head," to be presented to their deliverer, in the place of his name. Then shall the song be sung with raptures unknown before; "Lift up your heads, O "ye gates, and be ye lifted up, ye everlasting doors, and the king "of glory shall come in. Who is this king of glory? The Lord, "strong and mighty, the Lord, mighty in battle. The Lord of "hosts he is the king of glory. Selah." Psal. xxiv.

Shall a present be brought to JEHOVAH *of hosts.*] Oblations to God, the voluntary expressions of gratitude and affection, are services reasonable and acceptable. Such did Abel offer with tokens of divine regard. In this place it is evident from Isaiah, lxxvi. 20. That there is an allusion, to the yearly offering of the first fruits, among the Jews. These consisted of the earliest and most valuable productions of their fields, and of their flocks, as an acknowledgment, that to God they owed their harvest, and all their other enjoyments. In the same spirit the swift messengers, in evidence of their gratitude for their success, present the first and most excellent fruits of their labour, an oblation to Jehovah of hosts, on the day of his victory.

In ancient times, it was customary for cities, nations and individuals to offer golden crowns and other precious gifts to distinguished conquerors. The gifts were always in proportion, to their esteem of the conqueror, and the value they set on the splendor, and importance of his achievements.

What gift shall be offered to Zion's king? His dignity and his conquests are splendid and interesting beyond conception. The text describes the oblation and leaves astonishment astonished! An oblation of a people in numbers, in personal attractions, in talents, in estimation the most abject and contemptible which earth supported!

God himself, with a divine pencil, has drawn their picture and history, and experience attests, that the features are not overcharged. But they were now transformed. They had, by the ministry of the messengers, been raised from their graves. The spirit of God had reanimated them, and furnished them with new qualities, with new endowments. Their husband who is their maker, made them " look forth, as the morning, fair as the moon, " clear as the sun, and terrible as an army with banners."

Isaiah, transported, and overwhelmed, with the view, returns to their former character, as received from God, and contrasts it with their present condition. In the ardour of his soul, and the glow of his description, he omits, in the first member of the enumeration the preposition OF, for I cannot suppose with others, and that without evidence, and without necessity, that it has dropt from the original text.

" *A present of a people*, long dispersed and scattered among ' all the nations of men—Disowned by God—despised by the ' world—without personal charms—without talents, without gov-' ernment, temple, priest, magistrate, as unseemly to the eye as ' the stones and rubbish of their own temple—useless as branch-' es cut off from their Olive. Behold now a nation distinguish-' ed for personal and mental attractions, united in one body, the ' glorious centre, round which all the tribes of men rally, seated ' in the country of their Fathers, enjoying Zion, in all her gospel ' privileges with the son of the eternal a their royal head, and ' you must acknowledge, " This is the doings of the Lord, and " wonderous in our eyes."

A PRESENT OF A PEOPLE, " robbed, spoiled, snared in holes, " and hid in prison houses, a prey to every one, a prey whom " none delivered, in behalf of whom none said RESTORE." Behold this people, receiving now the wealth and the honours of the world. " The labour of Egypt, and the merchandize of Ethiopia " are theirs. Peace is extended to them like a river, and the " glory of the Gentiles like a flowing stream. They draw nour-" ishment from the breast of kings, they are borne on the sides, " they are dandled on the knees, as one who is comforted by his " mother, so God comforteth them. In Jerusalem shall he com-" fort them."

" *A present of a people*, on whom for ages, the terror of God
'and the dread of man, rested; a people who ceased not, to dis-
' cover restlessness and dismay in their countenance, and signs of
' continual apprehension of calamity and danger in their heart;
' a people who seemed to read enmity in every man's eye; and on
' whom the smile of friendship was never once kindled. Behold
' the change and admire the power and compassion of their once
' offended Jehovah. In composure of mind, and reposing unsus-
' pecting confidence, in God and in man, they appear within the sac-
' red enclosure of Zion. That blood that cried so long and so loud
' for vengeance and pursued them to the ends of the earth, now
' pleads for mercy and has driven all their fears away."

A present of a nation, heirs of expectation the most extensive and sublime, yet inheriting for so many years disappointed hopes in the extreme. They saw empires rise and disappear, they saw science blaze and science languish; revolution had under their eye succeeded revolution, but change in the moral or in the natural world afforded them not one ray of hope that their redemption was drawing near, that God was again to restore the kingdom to Israel, or that the hope of their fathers was advancing to visit them. Behold now, the hand of the Lord that bears the torch of day, causing " the day spring from on high to visit them." His proclamation has gone forth to the ends of the world, " saying, to " the daughter of Zion, behold thy salvation cometh, behold his " reward is with him, and his work before him, and they shall call " them the holy people, the redeemed of the Lord, and then Zion " shall be called, sought out, a city not forsaken." Isa. lxii. 11, 12.

A present of a nation trodden down, as the mire of the street, trampled under foot like the grape in the wine vat. God had made them as the " off scouring, and refuse in the midst of the people." The nations in violence eat them as bread, and poured out their blood like water on the earth. Behold the astonishing revolution in the sentiments of men, as soon as God hath demanded them as an oblation. " The sons of them that afflict them, " shall come bending unto them, and all they that despise them " shall bow themselves down at the soles of their feet, and they " shall call them, the people of the Lord, the Zion of the holy " one of Israel."

A PRESENT OF A NATION, whose country the rivers had spoiled. Over their country, as over themselves, wave after wave, and inundation succeeding inundation, had passed. Her very visage so marred, that, hardly one of her former fair and interesting features can be found. Her soil, like the flesh of one consumed by disease has wasted away. Her beautiful hills and her majestic mountains have become frightful, like the unshapely bones of a skeleton. Naked and bare, the eye recoils from the hideous and repulsive form. Vegetation herself as if affrighted refuses to ascend and to cover her naked shoulders and sides. The race of domestic animals and civilized tribes of men, have forsaken her. They have abandoned her once delightful abodes, to the obscene and howling beasts of the rocks and the forest ; or to bloody and ferocious Arabs, more vile and savage than they. Behold the change which that day shall witness,—A new earth is created. " The wilderness and the solitary place shall be glad " *for them*, and the desart shall rejoice and blossom as the rose. " It shall blossom abundantly, and rejoice with joy and singing. " The glory of Lebanon shall be given unto her, the excellency of " Carmel and Sharon. They shall see the glory of the Lord and " the excellency of our God." Isa. xxxiv. 1.

A change so great and so glorious must affect with joy and gladness every feeling and benevolent heart. Should the eye of a descendant of Jacob, meet these lines, they ought to fill him with rapture. It is for your nation that this scene is preparing. You love, you dearly love, your nation and the memory of faithful Abraham, and well you may ; turn your eye to his SEED, to him in whose day Abraham delighted ! Dare to take the gospels in your hand, compare them with the writings of your own seraphic prophet, your own unrivalled poet, and pass a just decision. We hear you exclaim Jesus of Nazareth, is Isaiah's virgin's son, the man of sorrows and the man that loved our nation, whom we have cruelly rejected !

To the place of the name, &c.] Zion is the place where the oblation shall be presented, accepted and lodged, with their king. For ages past, his name has been recorded there. Zion was the sacred depository of the records of all his deeds of wonder and of grace. On her east side, on those towering mountains, where, in her view, he achieved his recent victory of deathless fame, of fame which neither earth nor seas can bound. " Who can utter

ISAIAH CHAP. XVIII. V. 7.

"the mighty acts of the Lord? Who can show forth all his praise. His name shall endure for ever. His name shall be continued as long as the sun. Let the whole earth be filled with his glory, Amen and amen."

The persons who present the oblation are not mentioned, nor is there any need. They must be the same, to whom the charge was given above. They are thy swift messengers, O nation with the overshadowing wing.

But America shall not be alone in this arduous, in this honourable employment. Every nation, whose churches continue faithful to their Lord, shall send their sons, and employ their substance in this heaven-planned expedition. Britain and Denmark have already united in this laudable enterprize. "Surely the Isles, shall wait for me, and the ships of Tarshish first, to bring my sons from far, their silver and their gold with them, unto the name of the Lord thy God, and to the holy one of Israel, because he hath glorified thee!" Their white sails, their lofty prows, their equable and regular motion, their great numbers shall excite surprize. "Who are these that fly like doves to their windows," shall be re-echoed along Zion's shore. After the first fruits, a new set of messengers shall immediately depart from the field of battle, to gather in the remaining harvest. "And I will send those that escape of them unto the nation of *Tarshish*, (probably the East-Indies) to *Pul*, and *Lud* that draw the bow, to *Tubal* and *Javan* to the *Isles* afar off, that have not heard of my fame, neither have seen my glory, and they shall declare my glory among the Gentiles. And they shall bring all your brethren for an offering to the Lord, out of all nations, upon horses, and in chariots, and in litters, and upon mules, and upon swift beasts, to my holy mountain, Jerusalem, saith the the Lord, as the children of Israel bring an offering in a clean vessel, into the house of the Lord." Isa. lxvi. 19, 20.

To this the millenium state succeeds. A period fully and frequently predicted, but so faintly described, as to admonish us to say little, and speak with caution.

The following texts seem to comprize the substance of what God has thought proper to reveal.

"Ye shall go out with joy, and be led forth with peace; the mountains and the hills shall break forth into singing before you, and all the trees of the field shall clap their hands. Instead of the "thorn shall come up the fir tree, and instead of the briar, shall come up the myrtle tree, and it shall be to the Lord for a name, for an everlasting sign that shall not be cut off." Isa. lv. 13.

"The wolf also shall dwell with the lamb; and the leopard shall lie down with the kid; and the calf and the young lion, and the fatling together; and a little child shall lead them. And the cow and the bear shall feed; their young ones shall lie down together; and the lion shall eat straw like the ox. And the sucking child shall play on the hole of the asp, and the weaned child shall put his hand on the cockatrices' den. They shall not hurt nor destroy in all my holy mountain: for the earth shall be full of the knowledge of the Lord, as the waters cover the sea." Isa. xi. 6, 7, 8, 9.

I will rejoice in Jerusalem, and joy in my people, and the voice of weeping shall be no more heard in her; nor the voice of crying. *No more shall there be an infant of days; nor an old man that hath not filled his days. For he that dieth at an hundred years shall die a youth: and the sinner that dieth at an hundred years, shall be deemed accursed. For as the days of a tree: shall be the days of my people.* Isa. lxv. 19, 22.

In that happy state the Jews shall be as highly exalted as they are now depressed, and be esteemed more than any other nation beside. "Strangers shall stand and feed your flocks, and the sons of aliens shall be your plowmen, and vine dressers. But ye shall be named the PRIESTS of the Lord. Ye shall be called the MINISTERS of our God: Ye shall eat the riches of the Gentiles and in their glory shall ye boast yourselves. All that see them shall acknowledge them, that they are the SEED which the Lord hath BLESSED." Isa. lxi. 5, 6.

"And I saw an angel come down from heaven, having the key of the bottomless pit, and a great chain in his hand. And he laid hold on the dragon, that old serpent, which is the devil, and satan, and bound him a thousand years, and cast him into the bottomless pit, and shut him up and set a seal upon him, that he should deceive the nations no more till the thousand years should be fulfilled." Rev. xx. 1, 2, 3.

THE END.

POSTSCRIPT.

We subjoin the Translations of this chapter by Bishop *Lowth* and Bishop *Horsley.*

Bp. Lowth's Translation.

1. Ho! to the land of the winged Cymbal
Which borders on the rivers of Cush;
2. Which sendeth ambassadors on the sea,
And in vessels of Papyrus, on the face of the waters;
Go ye swift messengers,
To a nation stretched out in length and smoothed
To a people terrible from the first and hitherto,
A nation meted out by line and trodden down;
Whose land the rivers have nourished.
3. Yea, all ye that inhabit the world and that dwell on earth;
When the standard is lifted upon the mountains behold!
And when the trumpet is sounded hear!
4. For thus hath JEHOVAH said unto me
I will sit still, and regard my fixed habitation;
Like the clear heat after rain,
Like the dewy cloud in the day of harvest.
5. Surely before the vintage, when the bud is perfect;
And the blossom has become a swelling grape;
He shall cut off the shoots with pruning hooks,
And the branches he shall take away; he shall cut down.
6. They shall be left together, to the rapacious bird of the mountains:
And to the wild beasts of the earth:
And the rapacious bird shall summer upon it;
And every wild beast of the earth shall winter upon it.
7. At that time shall a gift be brought to JEHOVAH, the God of hosts,
From a people stretched out in length and smoothed,
And from a people terrible from the first and hitherto
A nation meted out by line and trodden down
Whose land rivers have nourished
To the place of the name of Jehovah God of
Hosts, to mount Zion.

Bp. Horsley's Translation.

1. Ho! land spreading wide the shadow of (thy) wings which are beyond the rivers of Cush.
2. Accustomed to send messengers by sea, even in bulrush vessels upon the surface of the waters! Go, swift messengers, unto a nation dragged away and plucked, unto a people wonderful from their beginning hitherto, a nation expecting, expecting, and trampled under foot, whose land rivers have spoiled:

3. All the inhabitants of the world, and dwellers upon earth, shall see the lifting up, as it were, of a banner upon the mountains; and shall hear the sounding, as it were, of a trumpet,
4. For thus saith JEHOVAH unto me; I will sit still, (but I will keep my eye upon my prepared habitation,) as the parching heat just before lightning, as the dewy cloud in the heat of harvest.
5. For, before the harvest, when the bud is coming to perfection, and the blossom has become a juicy berry, he will cut off the useless shoots with pruning hooks; and the bill shall take away the luxuriant branches.

6. They shall be left together to the bird of prey of the mountains, and to the beasts of the earth. And upon it shall the bird of prey summer, and all the beasts of the earth upon it shall winter.

7. At that season a present shall be led to JEHOVAH of hosts, a people dragged away and plucked; even of a people wonderful from their beginning hitherto: a nation expecting, expecting, and trampled under foot, whose land rivers have spoiled, unto the place of the name of JEHOVAH of hosts, Mount Zion.

Albany, May, 1814.

DISCOURSE

ON THE

RESTORATION OF THE JEWS:

DISCOURSE

ON THE

RESTORATION OF THE JEWS:

DELIVERED AT THE TABERNACLE, OCT. 28 AND DEC. 2, 1844.

BY M. M. NOAH.

With a Map of the Land of Israel.

NEW-YORK:
HARPER & BROTHERS, 82 CLIFF-STREET.

1845.

PREFACE.

Within a few years the attention of the Christian world has been directed, in a peculiar manner, to the character, condition, and future prospects of the Jewish people. Ministers of the Gospel, in more closely examining the predictions of the prophets, and the miraculous preservation of the chosen people, have been struck with the injustice and oppression they have met with for the last 1800 years; and how directly in opposition to the mild principles of the Gospel has this spirit of intolerance been carried out. The responsibility in being agents in this persecution, or even by passive acquiescence giving countenance to it, has at length awakened a just and apostolic feeling towards Israel, which has of late been manifested in a more enlarged and liberal consideration, both in the pulpit and in the domestic circle. True, the efforts to evangelize them, contrary, as I think, to the manifest predictions of the prophets, continue to be unceasing, yet even in this there is charity and good feelings which cannot fail to be reciprocally beneficial. In the political, as well as the religious world, there are singular commotions which point to the East as the theatre of approaching revolutions of great and absorbing interests, and it has struck me forcibly that a movement from this free country in favour of restoring the Jews to their ancient heritage would have the good effect of directing the attention of the Christian powers generally to an effort of this character, which might gradually lead to important results; but, at all events, would create a better and kinder feeling for the Jews, and secure to them protection and privileges which at present they do not all enjoy. If, in our generation, this movement does nothing more, it will accomplish much good, and would cement the ties which ought to unite the Jew and Christian in kind offices and brotherly love. There are also religious movements of great interest among the Jews in Europe —propositions of reform, which, if they do not strike at the religion itself, will do much good in wearing away ancient prejudices, and approximating to the enlightened spirit of the age. We require a Sanhedrin to examine many points and customs in our religion, and to compare the written with the oral law, and prune many excrescences in Rabbinical writings, some of which strike at the pure principles contained in the Bible, which, under all circumstances, is our safest guide. In the observations which I have made, and the facts detailed in relation to the great work of restoration, let it not be understood that I speak in the name and in behalf of the Jewish people throughout the world. Early religious dogmas cannot be changed; strong prejudices of education require time and perseverance to remove; the liberal mind alone will comprehend my views, and the objects I desire to attain. I seek to commit no one who differs with me; we are a sect, not a nation; there is no council, no government, as yet, through which opinions may be concentrated, consequently we are left to form our own opinions on disputed points. I confidently believe in the restoration of the Jews, and in the coming of the Messiah; and believing that political events are daily assuming a shape which may finally lead to that great advent, I considered it a duty to call upon the free people of this country to aid us in any efforts which, in our present position, it may be deemed prudent to adopt, and I have the most abiding confidence in their good-will and friendly feelings in aiding to restore us to liberty and independence.

In a letter which I received from Mr. Jefferson as far back as 1818, he observes, "Your sect, by its sufferings, has furnished a remarkable proof of the universal spirit of religious intolerance inherent in every sect, disclaimed by all while feeble, and practised by all when in power; our laws have applied the only antidote to this vice, protecting our religious as they do our civil rights, by putting all on an equal footing: but more remains to be done, for although we are free by the law, we are not so in practice; public opinion erects itself into an inquisition, and exercises its office with as much fanaticism as fans the flames of an *auto-da-fé*. The prejudice still scowling on your section of our religion, although the elder one, cannot be unfelt by yourselves. It is to be hoped that individual dispositions will at length mould themselves to the model of the law, and consider the moral basis on which all our religion rests as the rallying-point which unites them in a common interest, while the peculiar dogmas branching from it are the exclusive concern of the respective sects embracing them, and no rightful subject of notice to any other.

" Public opinion needs reformation on this point, which would have the farther happy effect of doing away the hypocritical maxim of '*intus ut lubet foris ut moris.*' Nothing, I think, would be so likely to effect this as to your sect particularly, as the more careful attention to education which you recommend, and which, placing its members on the equal and commanding benches of science, will exhibit them as equal objects of respect and favour."

In addition to the foregoing observations from the illustrious author of the Declaration of American Independence, I find similar and stronger sentiments in a letter from President John Adams, written to me when nearly in his ninetieth year, with all the fervour, sincerity, and zeal he exhibited in the early scenes of our Revolution. " You have not," says this venerable patriot, " extended your ideas of the right of private judgment and the liberty of conscience, both in religion and philosophy, farther than I do. Mine are limited only by morals and propriety. I have had occasion to be acquainted with several gentlemen of your nation, and to transact business with some of them, whom I found to be men of as liberal minds, as much honour, probity, generosity, and good breeding as any I have known in any sect of religion or philosophy.

"I wish your nation may be admitted to all the privileges of citizens in every part of the world. This country has done much; I wish it may do more, and annul every narrow idea in religion, government, and commerce. Let the wits joke, the philosophers sneer! What then? It has pleased the Providence of the 'first cause,' the universal cause, that Abraham should give religion not only to the Hebrews, but to Christians and Mohammedans, the greatest part of the modern civilized world."

In another letter Mr. Adams says, "I really wish the Jews again in Judea, an independent nation, for, as I believe, the most enlightened men of it have participated in the amelioration of the philosophy of the age; once restored to an independent government, and no longer persecuted, they would soon wear away some of the asperities and peculiarities of their character, possibly in time become liberal Unitarian Christians, for your Jehovah is our Jehovah, and your God of Abraham, Isaac, and Jacob is our God."

I cannot mistake the liberality of my countrymen in making to them the appeal I have made in the following pages. Their agency involves no responsibility, no outlay of money, no painful efforts: the project itself is pacific throughout; it places the Jews in the Holy Land as mere proprietors, protected in their possessions as other citizens and subjects—and this is the basis of the restoration. Other events will follow in their proper course.

This discourse was addressed to Christians, and I cannot express my gratification at the deep attention and liberal feelings manifested by some thousands of the most distinguished of our citizens and the highest dignitaries of the Church who heard me: it was a practical illustration of the real freedom of our institutions, and satisfied me that, where Church and State are not united, there is no barrier that separates religious sects, and all are alike free, liberal, and tolerant.

DISCOURSE, ETC.

I have long desired, my friends and countrymen, for an opportunity to appear before you in behalf of a venerable people, whose history, whose sufferings, and whose extraordinary destiny have, for a period of 4000 years, filled the world with awe and astonishment: a people at once the most favoured and the most neglected, the most beloved, and yet the most persecuted; a people under whose salutary laws all the civilized nations of the earth now repose; a people whose origin may date from the cradle of creation, and who are likely to be preserved to the last moment of recorded time.

I have been anxious to appeal to you, citizens and Christians, in behalf of the chosen and beloved people of Almighty God, to ask you to do justice to their character, to their motives, to their constancy, and to their triumphant faith; to feel for their sufferings and woes; to extend to them your powerful protection and undivided support in accomplishing the fulfilment of their destiny, and aiding to restore them to the land of their forefathers and the possession of their ancient heritage. It is, I acknowledge, a novel, though a natural appeal, made, I may say, for the first time to Christians since the advent of

Christianity; but the period, I believe, has arrived for this appeal: extraordinary events shadow forth results long expected, long prophesied, long ordained; commotions in the State and division in the Church; new theories put forth, new hopes excited, new promises made; and the political events in Syria, Egypt, Turkey, and Russia, indicate the approach of great and important revolutions, which may facilitate the return of the Jews to Jerusalem, and the organization of a powerful government in Judea, and lead to that millennium which we all look for, all hope for, all pray for.

Where, I ask, can we commence this great work of regeneration with a better prospect of success than in a free country and a liberal government? Where can we plead the cause of independence for the children of Israel with greater confidence than in the cradle of American liberty? Where ask for toleration and kindness for the seed of Abraham, if we find it not among the descendants of the Pilgrims? Here we can unfurl the standard, and seventeen millions of people will say, "God is with you; we are with you: in his name, and in the name of civil and religious liberty, go forth and repossess the land of your fathers. We have advocated the independence of the South American republics, we have given a home to our red brethren beyond the Mississippi, we have combated for the independence of Greece, we have restored the African to his native land. If these nations were entitled to our sympathies, how much more powerful and irrepressible are the claims of that beloved people, before whom the Almighty walked like a cloud by day and a pillar of fire by night; who spoke to them words of comfort and salvation, of promise, of hope, of consolation, and protection; who swore they should be *his* people, and he would be their God; who, for their special protection and final restoration, dispersed them among the nations of the earth, without confounding them with any!"

This, my countrymen, will be your judgment—your opinion—when asked to co-operate in giving freedom to the Jews. I am not required, on this occasion, to go over the history of the chosen people; you know it all; it is all recorded in that good Book which *we* have preserved for your comfort and consolation; that book which our fathers pressed to their hearts in traversing burning sands and the wide waste of waters, which famine, pestilence, and the sword could not wrest from them; which was the last cherished relic at night, and the first precious gift in the morning. You will find their history in the Bible.

We are the only people who can trace our pedigree to the infancy of nature, the only nation to whom a code of just and righteous laws were confided. Compare our situation with that of the various nations among whom we have lived, and we at once trace the cause of all our unhappiness. Our father Abraham was the first to proclaim the unity of God, Sovereign Architect of the world, Ruler of heaven and earth. Joseph, fourth descendant of Abraham, carried the same doctrines and religion with him among the Egyptians; honoured by Pharaoh, but hated by the people, who revenged themselves by violence and persecutions on his posterity. Moses, our great lawgiver, delivered them from the yoke of their oppressors, and conveyed them to the frontier of the promised land. Joshua, commanding the armies of Israel, entered the land of Canaan, planted his standard there, and the world beheld for the first time a regular code of civil, political, and religious laws, which exist even at this day in all their primitive force. Solomon, the third king of Israel, by his wisdom and glory advanced the people and country to the highest degree of splendour in arts, in arms, and in science; in wealth, in commerce, and letters; and created those jealousies among the neighbouring nations which led to wars, intestine commotions, and, finally, to the loss of the holy city, which fell into the hands of the Romans, and from that period Israel ceased to be a nation, and became scattered over the face of the earth.

The deep-rooted hatred of the ancient nations of the Israelites is therefore traceable to one great cause. Egypt, the worshippers of an ox or a crocodile, could not love a people who acknowledged only the true God. The Greeks, who murdered Socrates because he taught the existence of that God, equally detested the Jews, who openly proclaimed his unity and omnipotence. The idolatrous Canaanites, the conquered and defeated race, abhorred the Jews for their religious opinions. The Romans, who believed in oracles, soothsayers, and auguries, were always their fierce and irreconcilable enemies. We account, therefore, for the hatred of those nations who, attached to their idols, were the persecutors of the Jews; but how are we to account for the oppression we have met with from our Christian brethren, having the same origin with us, our fellow-sufferers under Nero, Vespasian, Titus, and others? Let me probe the causes to their very foundation, by showing the errors of the first era of the Christian Church, and the departure from the injunctions, morality, charity, and good-will of the primitive founders of that faith.

I approach the subject, my countrymen, I trust, in a becoming spirit of respect for the attachment and devotion to the Christian faith of those who now hear me. Born and educated among Christians—having, through their confidence and liberality, held various stations of public trust—I bring to the consideration of this deeply-absorbing subject the most kind and apostolic feeling. Tinctured by no prejudice, governed by no ill will, controlled by no bigoted impulse, but with an enlarged and upright zeal, and a desire to promote human happiness equally among all faiths, I will endeavour to explain, for the first time in many centuries, how the chosen people understand and interpret the advent of Christianity, its application to them as a nation, the influence it has had on their destiny, and their views of its obligations.

We have the authority of early writers, of eminent Christian divines, of illustrious scholars and historians, for the declaration so often preached, until it is generally believed, that all the calamities of the Jews, their persecutions and sufferings, their degradation as a nation, their outcast and despised condition in many countries even at this day, are the results of the agency our fathers had in compassing the death of Jesus of Nazareth. We are, it has been said by them, crushed beneath the cross, and our only salvation is in believing in the divinity of him whom our forefathers had rejected. Hence the great, and eager, and natural desire to evangelize the Jews, and thus atone for what is deemed among pious Christians that great sin.

Let us calmly examine this subject. Let us look at the peculiar position of the Jewish nation when those important events occurred, and ascertain by what agencies and motives they were governed and influenced.

The sins of the chosen people, principally idolatry, for which they were denounced by the prophets, and punished by the Almighty, occurred before the Babylonish captivity; since that time those peculiar sins have not been repeated, and their constancy and fidelity as a nation, to their faith and principles, remain unquestioned at this day. The immense power and glory of the Jewish nation under David and Solomon long excited, as I have already said, the envy of surrounding nations. The return of the Jews to Palestine under the decree of Cyrus, at which epoch the history of the Old Testament closes, found them in a feeble condition under the Persian kings, and the entire people at one period were in danger of being destroyed by the cruel edict of Ahasuerus; and their unsettled position, together with the decay of their influence, gave rise to several divisions and sects, which greatly impaired their harmony and unity as a nation. The Persian Empire was at length subdued by Alexander the Great, 208 years after its conquest by Cyrus. The Jews attached themselves, with their usual fidelity, to Darius, and Alexander, exasperated at their decision in favour of his rival, marched upon Jerusalem; but, struck with the imposing character of their venerable faith, became their friend and protector, gave them many privileges, and selected several of the most distinguished as first settlers in his new city of Alexandria. On the death of Alexander, and the division of the empire among four of his generals, Judea became the theatre of war and intestine commotion, division and troubles of all kinds, cruelty, carnage, and oppression, until the Asmonean family, lamenting with deep anguish the wretched condition of their country and brethren, resolved to strike a blow for liberty, and for many years Judas Maccabees and brothers triumphed over their enemies, restored peace to Jerusalem, beautified the sanctuary, and enforced obedience to the Divine Law.

At length, after many trials and reverses, the Romans, under Pompey, laid siege to and captured Jerusalem, and the Jews passed under the Roman yoke, and all that was left to the chosen people was the privilege to pursue their religion unmolested; and, after unparalleled sufferings, Herod the Idumenean ascended the throne of Judea, persecuted and oppressed the people, and rendered himself so odious, that, to retrieve something of his former standing, he rebuilt the Temple with great splendour, but, as an acknowledgment of his tributary position, set up a golden eagle over the gates of the sanctuary. It was at this period, when the Jews had lost all power as a nation; when, broken down and dispirited, and but a shadow of their former liberty and glory remained to them; when it needed no prophetic warning to denote the final overthrow of the nation, that Jesus of Nazareth was born. They had expected some one at that period who was destined to act as their Messiah and temporal deliverer; some one who could break the Roman yoke, and change the aspect of human affairs; they sighed for liberty and vengeance, and prayed devoutly for a deliverer. Jesus of Nazareth was not the one they expected. His mission of peace and spirit of reform held forth no temporal hope to the afflicted. He had no sword or helmet to indicate the warrior or conqueror; he unfurled no banner, sounded no trumpet, prophesied no victory over the pagans, and the Jews gave themselves up to despair.

To comprehend and fully understand the peculiar situation in which the Jewish people were placed at that important crisis, we must endeavour, if possible, to place ourselves in their position. A nation once powerful, rich, and happy, prosperous and independent, the conquerors of every neighbouring power, living in the midst of luxury and civilization, enjoying a happy and equitable code of laws, with wise kings, gallant warriors, a pious priesthood, and great national prosperity, suddenly assailed by powerful pagan nations, allured by a love of gold, and tempted by the hope of plunder, contending year after year against fearful odds, their enemy strengthened by fresh levies, while their own resources were exhausted, finding themselves at length gradually sinking, a weak, decayed, defeated power, the once glorious and favoured people abandoned by hope and almost deserted by Providence, their Temple, their pride and glory, wrested from them, and the beams of the setting sun falling on the brazen helmet of the Roman centurion keeping guard near the Holy of Holies. In this distracted position, and at this period of unexampled calamity, Jesus of Nazareth found the Jews at the commencement of his ministry.

Corruptions, the natural consequence of great misfortune, had crept in among them: a portion of the priesthood forgot the obligations due to their high order; hypocrisy and intrigue had reached the high places, and Jesus appeared among them the most resolute of reformers. Denouncing the priests and Pharisees, preaching against hypocrisy and vice, prophesying the downfall of the nation, and in thus attracting followers and apostles by his extraordinary and gifted powers, he became formidable by his decision of character, his unceremonious expression of opinion, and the withering nature of his rebuke. He preached at all times and at all places, in and out of the Temple, with an eloquence such as no mortal has since possessed, and, to give the most powerful and absorbing interest to his mission, he proclaimed himself Son of God, and declared himself ordained by the Most High to save a benighted and suffering people, as their Saviour and Redeemer. The Jews were amazed, perplexed, and bewildered at all they saw and heard. They knew Jesus from his birth. He was in constant intercourse with his brethren in their domestic relations, and surrounded by their household gods; they remembered him a boy, disputing, as was the custom, most learnedly with the doctors in the Temple; and yet he proclaimed himself the Son of God, and performed, as it is said, most wonderful miracles, was surrounded by a number of disciples of poor but extraordinarily gifted men, who sustained his doctrines, and had an abiding faith in his mission; he gathered strength and followers as he progressed; he denounced the whole nation, and prophesied its destruction, with their altars and temples; he preached against whole cities, and proscribed their leaders with a force which, even at this day, would shake our social systems. The Jews became alarmed at his increasing power and influence, and the Sanhedrin resolved to become his accuser, and bring him to trial under the law, as laid down in the 13th of Deuteronomy.

In reflecting deeply on all the circumstances of this, the most remarkable trial and judgment in history, I am convinced, from the whole tenour of the proceedings, that the arrest, trial, and condemnation of Jesus of Nazareth was conceived and executed under a decided panic. That he proclaimed himself Son of God; that he declared he had been delegated from the Father to enter upon his mediatorial character, that he was a prophet, and the promised Messiah, was understood and admitted by all his friends and disciples; but still, it has appeared to me throughout that there was not sufficient testimony to come under the special and distinct provisions of the Law.

The parables and figures of the Hebrew language, and the Oriental mode of expression, frequently cloud and embarrass the real meaning intended to be conveyed. Jesus uniformly acknowledged the unity and omnipotence of God; to Him he prayed, as our Father in heaven, whose name was hallowed, whose will was to be executed on eartn; he disclaimed any intention to alter the Mosaic Law, but confirmed and observed every part of it. Take, for example, one fact, for so it will be considered, which we find in the twelfth chapter of St. Mark, the twenty-ninth verse, in reply to a question put to Him by one of the scribes, as to which is the first commandment of all. "And Jesus answered him, The first of all the commandments is, Hear, O Israel, the Lord our God is one Lord." With these words on his lips, with this belief in his heart, it is impossible to have convicted him of blasphemy. It is our creed, our universal prayer, the basis of our faith; how could such a declaration have been construed into blasphemy? The title of God was a title of power and dominion, and frequently was conferred by the Almighty himself on earthly rulers. "See, I have made thee a God to Pharaoh," as God Supreme said to Moses; "Son of God" was a title frequently conferred on those of distinguished piety and learning, and on those possessing the emanations of the Divinity; and this title the apostles themselves carry out in all their writings.

"THE SON," "*My* Son," not the Father; the humanity, not the Divinity; the *image* of the invisible God, not the invisible God himself; and Paul says, there is one God and one Mediator between God and man. Could the Almighty delegate a mediatorial character to any on earth? who can doubt it? God says to Moses, "Behold, I send an angel before thee to keep thee in the way; provoke him not, for he will not pardon your transgressions, for my name is in him—my spirit is in him."

It was not, therefore, altogether on the charge of Jesus having called himself Son of God that the Sanhedrin accused and condemned him; political considerations mingled themselves, and in a measure controlled the decision of the council, and this is demonstrable from the declaration of Caiaphas himself, as stated in the Gospel, "Better that one man should die than the nation should be destroyed."

"It was the sedition, and not altogether the blasphemy—the terror and apprehension of political overthrow, which led to conviction, and this political and national characteristic was maintained throughout; it was that consideration which induced the Jews to urge upon Pilate a confirmation of the sentence. It was the charge of assuming the prerogatives of Cæsar, not the name of the Divinity, which overcame the well-founded objections of the Roman governor, and crucifixion itself was a Roman and not a Jewish punishment. The opprobrious insults heaped upon the Master came from Roman soldiers, and that mixed rabble which even in our days desecrate all that is held sacred.

I place these most absorbing events before you, my countrymen, as I find them recorded in the New Testament, not to contrast things sacred with those which are profane, but that you should understand the exact position of the Jews at that time, their painful situation, their prostrate condition, their timidity, their agitation, without even a ray of hope; a people so venerable for their antiquity, so beloved and protected for their fidelity, on the very threshold of political destruction.

It is not my duty to condemn the course of our ancestors, nor yet to justify the measures they adopted in that dire extremity; but if there are mitigating circumstances, I am bound by the highest considerations which a love of truth and justice dictates, to spread them before you, at the same time to protest against entailing upon us the responsibility of acts committed eighteen hundred years ago by our fathers, and thus transmit to untold generations the anger and hatred of a faith erroneously taught to believe us the aggressors. True, it may be said that the Jews declared their willingness to let the blood of Jesus be on their heads and the heads of their children. I do maintain that the assumption of responsibility in that case extended only to them and to their children. In the Commandments, God visits the iniquities of the father on the children to the third and fourth generation, and then only to those who hate him: who can have the power to go beyond the limits for the punishment of sin, real or imaginary, express or implied, which God himself has ordained? All the persecutions which the Jews have suffered at the hands of Christians have arose from the injustice of making one generation answerable for the acts of another.

The Jews, my friends, were but the instruments of a higher power, and in rejecting Jesus of Nazareth we have a great and overwhelming evidence of the infinite wisdom of the Almighty. Had they acknowledged him as their Messiah at that fearful crisis, the whole nation would have gradually sunk under the Roman yoke, and we should have had at this day paganism and idolatry, with all their train of terrible evils, and darkness and desolation would have been spread over the face of the earth. But the death of Jesus was the birth of Christianity; the Gentile Church sprang from the ruins which surrounded its primitive existence; its march was onward, beset with darkness and difficulties, with oppression and persecution, until the sun of the Reformation rose upon it, dissipating the clouds of darkness which had obscured its beauties, and it shone forth with a liberal and tolerant brightness, such as the Great Master had originally designed it.

Had not that event occurred, how would you have been saved from your sins? The Jews, in this, did nothing but what God himself ordained, for you will find it written in the Acts of your Apostles, "And now, brethren, I know that through ignorance ye did it, as did also your rulers."

It has been said, and with some commendations on what was called my liberality, that I did not in this discourse, on its first delivery, term Jesus of Nazareth an impostor—I have never considered him such. The impostor generally aims at temporal power, attempts to subsidize the rich and weak believer, and draws around him followers of influence whom he can control. Jesus was free from fanaticism; his was a quiet, subdued, retiring faith; he mingled with the poor, communed with the wretched, avoided the rich, and rebuked the vainglorious. In the calm of the evening he sought shelter in the secluded groves of Olivet, or wandered pensively on the shores of Galilee. He sincerely believed in his mission; he courted no one, flattered no one; in his political denunciations he was pointed and severe, in his religion calm and subdued. These are not characteristics of an impostor; but, admitting that we give a different interpretation to his mission, when 150 millions believe in his Divinity, and we see around us abundant evidences of the happiness, good faith, mild government, and liberal feelings which spring from his religion, what right has any one to call him an impostor? That religion which is calculated to make mankind great and happy cannot be a false one.

While the Almighty raised up, enlarged, and extended the Gentile Church, gave to it power and dominion, he threw the mantle of his Divine protection over his chosen people, and has preserved them amid unheard-of dangers to this very day, numerous as they have been, but still distinct as a nation, preserving the Abrahamic covenant, walking in his statutes, and obeying his commandments; the same people whom he had brought out of Egyptian bondage, and to whom he had given the land of Israel as an inheritance for ever, and who is now leading us back in peace and happiness to repossess our ancient and promised heritage. Can the human mind imagine a miracle such as this which we have before us? Do you now perceive, Christians and brethren, why it was not designed by the Almighty that the Jews at that crisis should have acknowledged the Messiahship of Jesus of Nazareth? " The secret things are for the Lord."

Fully appreciating, therefore, as I do, the pious and benevolent objects of the Society for Evangelizing the Jews throughout the world, and desirous that those societies should continue to feel an interest both in the temporal and eternal welfare of Israel, I do not think—pardon me for saying—that their success has been commensurate with the great efforts they have made, and the means expended in the advancement of the objects in view. My desire now is, that, feeling the same interest, and directed by the same zeal, those societies should unite in efforts to promote the restoration of the Jews in their *unconverted* state, relying on the fulfilment of the prophecies and the will of God for attaining the objects they have in view after that great advent shall have arrived

A change of religious faith, even among the least faithful, is a plant of slow progress; but among a people specially chosen and signally preserved amid the ruins of the world and the downfall of every other nation of antiquity, is an effort of insurmountable difficulty. It is impolitic to send converted Jews to preach Christianity to Israel. However sincere they may be, they never inspire confidence among their brethren. A distrust in their sincerity precedes every effort they may make. Equally impolitic—I say it respectfully—was the appointment of a converted Jew as Bishop of Jerusalem, to commence his labours of conversion on a spot so dear to the Jews, to which they are so faithfully, so devotedly, so sincerely attached; a place to which they journey in their last pilgrimage to die *as* Jews, and be buried near their kings, prophets, and judges in the valley of Jehoshaphat. If your efforts are still to be devoted to evangelizing as well as restoring, send pious and sincere Christians to them, who entertain a kind and benevolent feeling for the Jews; and if they should not succeed in accomplishing all they desire, the messengers, at least, will be well, and kindly, and courteously received, and their mission treated with confidence and regard.

But a difficulty presents itself in the work of evangelizing which probably has not heretofore occurred to you. Let us suppose it to be as successful as the labourers in the vineyard would desire, what church is to receive us? If we join the Protestant, the Catholic will say, "We are the elder brother of the Christian Church; we spring from your fathers; the first fifteen bishops of our Church were Jews; we separated under the walls of Jerusalem, and, after a painful pilgrimage of 1800 years, if you are satisfied to believe in what we believe, come to us, to the communion of saints, to the remission of sins." The Protestants will say, in their usual mild and tolerant spirit, " We keep pace with the enlightened spirit of the age: here is the Bible, which was intrusted to your safe keeping, and we restore it to you unchanged; with us you will find that liberality and charity go hand in hand, free from idolatry, from the remnants of paganism, free from the control of temporal power." The Unitarian will say, " *In medio tutissimus.*' Come to our Church, thou pillar which standest alone amid the destruction of empires; we believe with you in the unity and omnipotence of God; we do not ask you to abandon the laws of Moses, should you ever adopt the Gospel of Jesus. Come with us." The Methodist, the Presbyterian, the Universalist, the Baptist, the Socinian, the Quaker, and other churches, each have peculiar doctrines. I complain not of this: in the multitude of sects there is safety; but how are we to choose? In the divisions of the Christian Church, how are we to find the true one? I stood recently in front of a noble church in a neighbouring city, adorned with all the splendour of architecture, and all the embellishments of pious taste. It was surrounded by a frightful mob, which had set fire to it. They brandished their incendiary torches, and threw them flashing in the middle of the aisles; they covered the altar with straw, and heaped it with missals and hymn-books. The flames spread rapidly in every direction, until they reached and curled round a magnificent altar-piece —a triumph of the art. The whole church was one bright sheet of fire: the devouring element stormed, and rushed, and roared, until it encompassed the broad and stately dome. I saw the golden cross by which it was surmounted encircled with myriads of bright sparks, while the flames played round its base—that cross, *In hoc signo vincit*, melting before the consuming heat. At length the whole dome fell, and cinders, murky clouds, and flames ascended high in air: then the ruffians sent up a shout which gave alarm to the host of heaven —a shout of exultation that a Christian church, in a land of religious freedom, had been destroyed by men calling themselves Christians. This is one of the stumbling-blocks to the Jews which we cannot overleap, though in our way it lies. When did the chosen people ever fire any structure raised to the honour of God?

But, my friends, why not ask yourselves the great and cardinal question whether it is not your duty to aid in restoring the chosen people as Jews to their promised land? Are we not the only witnesses of the unity and omnipotence of God? Are we not the only witnesses of the truth of the Bible, preserved as such by the great Sovereign Architect of the world? The predictions of the restoration of Israel, distinctly intimated by prophecy, are as full as were the predictions of our overthrow and desolation. Has not God threatened and punished, and will not his promises of favour be fulfilled? Has he cast off his people, or has he merely visited their transgressions with punishment? " Behold," saith the Lord, " I will take the children of Israel from among the heathen whither they be gone, and will gather them on every side, and bring them into their own land, and I will make them one nation, in the land upon the mountains of Israel. Then shall they know that I am the Lord their God, which caused them to be led into captivity among the heathen: but I have gathered them into their own land, and have left none of them any more there. Neither will I hide my face any more from them, for I have poured out my Spirit upon the house of Israel, saith the Lord. Thus the redeemed of the Lord shall return, and come with singing into Zion; they shall obtain gladness and joy, and sorrow and mourning shall flee away. Then shall Jerusalem be a crown of glory in the hand of the Lord; she shall no more be termed forsaken, nor her land be termed desolate.'

In almost every page of the Bible we have, directly and indirectly, in positive language and in parables the literal assurance and guarantee for the restoration of the Jews to Judea. We have gone through the fiery ordeal according to prediction; we have suffered the curses, and now await the period of the blessings. The past has been dark and dreary, the future is full of hope and splendour. God himself has been our ruler, our lawgiver, our leader, and to this hour our true friend. In the midst of appalling dangers his eye has been upon us, his protecting shield has been before us. To us he committed the lamp which has illumined the world, and we have held it with a steady hand for a light to the Gentiles.

No, no, my friends; what would be to us our blessings, our redemption, our salvation, without our restoration? Our land is blighted with the curse, shall it not enjoy the blessing? It long hath mourned, shall it not rejoice?

Innumerable are the promises which present themselves wherever the eye is turned. " The remnant of Jacob," saith the prophet, " shall be in the midst of many people, as a dew from the Lord, as showers upon the grass." And Isaiah, rapt in the contemplation of the glorious future reserved for his brethren of the Jewish Church, says, " Lift up thine eyes round about and see: all they gather themselves together, they come to thee: thy sons shall come from afar, and thy daughters shall be nursed at thy side."

We find the current strong and impulsive in every chapter of that illustrious prophet. " And the Lord shall set up an ensign for the nations, and shall assemble the outcasts of Israel, and gather together the dispersed of Judah from the four corners of the earth. Cry out and shout, inhabitants of Zion, for great is the Holy One of Israel in the midst of thee."

Again: listen to the prophet relative to the restoration and the rebuilding of Zion. "Behold, I will gather them out of all countries whither I have driven them in my anger, and in my fury, and in great wrath, and I will bring them again to this place, and I will cause them to dwell safely, and they shall be my people, and I will be their God, and I will make with them an *everlasting* covenant, and I will *not* turn away from them to do them good, and I will plant them in thy land, assuredly with my whole heart, and with my whole soul: for thus saith the Lord, Like as I have brought all this great evil upon this people, so will I bring them all the good that I have promised them. I, the Lord, have called thee in righteousness, and will hold thine hand, and will keep thee, and give thee for a covenant of the people, for *a light of the Gentiles:* I am the Lord. *That* is my name, and my glory I will not give to another." "Fear not, for I am with thee; be not dismayed, for I am thy God. Behold, all that were incensed against thee shall be ashamed and confounded. Arise, shine, for thy light *is* come, and the glory of the Lord is risen upon thee, and the Gentiles shall come to thy light, and kings to the brightness of thy rising." "Whereas thou hast been forsaken and hated, so that no man went through thee, I will make thee an *eternal* excellency, a joy of many generations. Violence shall no more be heard in thy land, wasting nor destruction within thy borders, but thou shalt call thy walls salvation, and thy gates praise. Thy people, also, shall be all righteous; they shall inherit the land *forever*. The branch of my planting, the work of my hands, that I may be glorified. And the sons of strangers shall build up thy walls, and their kings shall minister unto thee; for in my wrath I smote thee, but in my favour I had mercy upon thee. For the nation and kingdom that will not serve thee shall perish, and I will bless them that bless thee, and curse them that curse thee."

On these unfulfilled predictions, my friends, rest the happiness of the human race; and you are heirs to this new covenant, partners in the compact, sharers in the glory. Understand these prophecies distinctly: they relate to the literal, and not to the spiritual restoration of the Jews, as many believe. Some think that these prophecies were fulfilled at the restoration from Babylon; but you will find in the eleventh of Isaiah, beginning at the eleventh verse, these words: "And it shall come to pass in that day, that the Lord shall set his hand *again* the *second* time to recover the remnant of his people, which will be left (not in Babylon, but) from Assyria, and from Egypt, and from Pathros, and from Cush, and from Elam, and from Shina, and from

Hamath, and from the islands of the sea"—the whole world.

Above all, you that believe in the predictions of your apostles—you who believe in the second coming of the Son of Man—where is he to come to? By your own showing, to Jerusalem, to Zion, to the beloved city of hope and promise; He is, according to your own evangelists, to your own belief, to come to the Jews, and yet you would convert them *here;* you strive to evangelize them, in the face of all that is sacred in the promises of God and the predictions of his prophets, that they shall occupy their own land *as Jews.* In your zeal you forget the solemn, emphatic, brief declaration of your Redeemer, which you should remember as the shades of darkness draw around you, and the light of morning breaks upon your sight, "*Salvation is of the Jews.*"

Within the last twenty-five years great revolutions have occurred in the East, affecting in a peculiar manner the future destiny of the followers of Mohammed, and distinctly marking the gradual advancement of the Christian power. Turkey has been deprived of Greece, after a fearful and sanguinary struggle, and the land of warriors and sages has become sovereign and independent. Egypt conquered and occupied Syria, and her fierce pacha had thrown off allegiance to the sultan. Menaced, however, by the superior power of the Ottoman Porte, Mehemet Ali was compelled to submit to the

E

commander of the faithful, reconveying Syria to Turkey, and was content to accept the hereditary possession of Egypt.

Russia has assailed the wandering hordes of the Caucasses. England has had various contests with the native princes of India, and has waged war with China. The issue of these contests in Asia has been marked with singular success, and evidently indicate the progressive power of the Christian governments in that interesting quarter of the globe. France has carried its victorious arms through the north of Africa. Russia, with a steady glance and firm step, approaches Turkey in Europe, and when her railroads are completed to the Black Sea, will pour in her Cossacks from the Don and the Vistula, and Constantinople will be occupied by the descendants of the Tartar dynasty, and all Turkey in Europe, united to Greece, will constitute either an independent empire, or be occupied by Russia, who, with one arm on the Mediterranean, and the other on the North Sea, will nearly embrace all Europe. The counterbalance of this gigantic power will be a firm and liberal union of Austria with all Italy and the Roman States, down to the borders of Gaul: but the revolution will not end here. England must possess Egypt, as affording the only secure route to her possessions in India through the Red Sea; then Palestine, thus placed between the Russian possessions and Egypt, reverts to its legitimate proprietors, and for the safety of the surrounding nations, a powerful, wealthy, independent, and enterprising people are placed there by and with the consent of the Christian powers, and with their aid and agency the land of Israel passes once more into the possession of the descendants of Abraham. The ports of the Mediterranean will be again opened to the busy hum of commerce; the fields will again bear the fruitful harvest, and Christian and Jew will together, on Mount Zion, raise their voices in praise of Him whose covenant with Abraham was to endure forever, and in whose seed all the nations of the earth are to be blessed. This is our destiny. Every attempt to colonize the Jews in other countries has failed: their eye has steadily rested on their own beloved Jerusalem, and they have said, " The time will come, the promise will be fulfilled."

The Jews are in a most favourable position to repossess themselves of the promised land, and organize a free and liberal government; they are at this time zealously and strenuously engaged in advancing the cause of education. In Poland, Moldavia, Wallachia, on the Rhine and Danube, and wherever the liberality of the governments have not interposed obstacles, they are practical farmers. Agriculture was once their only natural employment; the land is now desolate, according to the prediction of the prophets, but it is full of hope and promise. The soil is rich, loamy, and everywhere indicates fruitfulness, and the magnificent cedars of

Lebanon, show the strength of the soil on the highest elevations; the climate is mild and salubrious, and double crops in the low lands may be annually anticipated. Everything is produced in the greatest variety. Wheat, barley, rye, corn, oats, and the cotton plant in great abundance. The sugar-cane is cultivated with success; tobacco grows plentifully on the mountains; indigo is produced in abundance on the banks of the Jordan; olives and olive oil are everywhere found; the mulberry almost grows wild, out of which the most beautiful silk is made; grapes of the largest kind flourish everywhere; cochineal is procured in abundance on the coast, and can be most profitably cultivated. The coffee-tree grows almost spontaneously; and oranges, figs, dates, pomegranates, peaches, apples, plums, nectarines, pineapples, and all the tropical fruits known to us, flourish everywhere throughout Syria. The several ports in the Mediterranean which formerly carried on a most valuable commerce can be advantageously reoccupied. Manufactures of wool, cotton, and silk could furnish all the Levant and the islands of the Mediterranean with useful fabrics. In a circumference within twenty days' travel of the Holy City, two millions of Jews reside. Of the two and a half tribes which removed east of the trans-Jordanic cities, Judah and Benjamin, and half Manasseh, I compute the number in every part of the world as exceeding six millions. Of the missing nine and a half tribes, part of which are in Turkey, China, Hindostan, Persia, and on this Continent, it is impossible to ascertain their numerical force. Many retain only the strict observance of the Mosaic laws, rejecting the Talmud and Commentaries. Others, in Syria, Egypt, and Turkey, are rigid observers of all the ceremonies. Reforms are in progress which correspond with the enlightened character of the age, without invading any of the cardinal principles of the religion. The whole sect are therefore in a position, as far as intelligence, education, industry, undivided enterprise, variety of pursuits, science, a love of the arts, political economy, and wealth could desire, to adopt the initiatory steps for the organization of a free government in Syria, as I have before said, by, and with the consent, and under the protection of the Christian powers. I propose, therefore, for all the Christian societies who take an interest in the fate of Israel, to assist in their restoration by aiding to colonize the Jews in Judea; the progress may be slow, but the result will be certain. The tree must be planted, and it will not want liberal and pious hands to water it, and in time it may flourish and produce fruit of hope and blessing.

The first step is to solicit from the Sultan of Turkey permission for the Jews to purchase and hold land; to build houses, and to follow any occupation they may desire, without molestation and in perfect security. There is no difficulty in securing this privilege for them. The moment the Christian powers feel an interest in behalf of the Jewish people, the Turkish government will secure and carry out their views, for it must always be remembered that the one hundred and twenty millions of Mussulmen are also the descendants of Abraham. There is but a single link that divides us, and they also are partners in the great compact. The Jews are, at this day, the most influential persons connected with the commerce and monetary affairs of Turkey, and enjoy important privileges, but hitherto they have had no protecting influence, no friendly hand stretched forth to aid them. The moment the sultan issues his *Hatti Scherif*, allowing the Jews to purchase and hold land in Syria, subject to the same laws and limitations which govern Mussulmen, the whole territory surrounding Jerusalem, including the villages Hebron, Safat, Tyre, also Beyroot, Jaffa, and other ports of the Mediterranean, will be occupied by enterprising Jews. The valleys of the Jordan will be filled by agriculturists from the north of Germany, Poland, and Russia. Merchants will occupy the seaports, and the commanding positions within the walls of Jerusalem will be purchased by the wealthy and pious of our brethren. Those who desire to reside in the Holy Land, and have not the means, may be aided by these societies to reach their desired haven of repose. Christians can thus give impetus to this important movement; and emigration flowing in, and actively engaged in every laudable pursuit, will soon become consolidated, and lay the foundation for the elements of government and the triumph of restoration. This, my friends, may be the glorious result of any liberal movement you may be disposed to make in promoting the final destiny of the chosen people.

The discovery and application of steam will be found to be a great auxiliary in the promotion of this interesting experiment. Steam packets to Alexandria leave England every fortnight; a line of packets are established between Marseilles and Constantinople, stopping at the Italian ports, and at Athens and Smyrna, thus bringing the Jewish people within a few days' travel of Jerusalem. Our Mediterranean and Levant trade, hitherto much neglected, will be revived, affording facilities to reach Palestine from this country direct.

While many who are now present may suppose that we shall not live to hear of the triumphant success of this project, yet, my friends, it may be nearer than we imagine. Let us unfurl the standard, leaving the result to Him whose protecting influence overshadows us all—who is infinite in wisdom, unbounded and unrestricted in power. The Jews suppose that the period of the restoration, which they so ardently desire and pray for, must be determined by the will of God alone, and that their agency in bringing about this great advent is not required, and, consequently, they wait patiently, without making those preliminary efforts so essential to the consummation of that great object. We never yet have been fully sensible of our duties and obligations as agents of a higher Power. Providence has endowed us with mind, with reason, with energy; blessed us with ample means to carry out his expressed wishes, laws, and ordinances. If we do not move when he disposes events to correspond with the fulfilment of his promises and the prediction of his prophets, we leave undone that which he entails upon us as a duty to perform, and the work is not accomplished, the day of deliverance has not arrived. He has spoken—he has promised. It is our duty, if the fulfilment of that Divine promise can be secured by mortal means and human agency, to see it executed. Will the dews of heaven produce a harvest without the labour of the husbandman?

But we cannot move alone in the great work of the restoration. The power and influence of our Christian brethren, which now control the destinies of the world, must be invoked in carrying out this most interesting project.

I am persuaded that the great events connected with the millennium so confidently predicted in the Scriptures, so anxiously desired by liberal and pious Christians, so intimately blended with the latter days—that consummation of a great and providential design in the union of the Jews and Gentiles, and the fulfilment of the prophecies—can alone be looked for *after* the restoration of the Jews to the land which the Lord gave to them for an everlasting possession. It is your duty, men and Christians, to aid us peaceably, tranquilly, and triumphantly to repossess the land of our fathers, to which we have a legal, equitable, perpetual right, by a covenant which the whole civilized world acknowledges. That power and glory which were once our own, you now possess; the banner of the Crescent floats where the standard of Judah was once displayed: it is for you to unfurl it again on Mount Zion. It will redound to your honour—it will perpetuate your glory. You believe in the second coming of Jesus of Nazareth. That second advent, Christians, depends upon you. It cannot come to pass, by your own admission, until the Jews are restored, and restored in their unconverted state. If he is again to appear, it must be to his own people, and in the land of his birth and his affections—on the spot where he preached, and prophesied, and died.

From the days of Constantine, when Church and State were first united, when the Christian religion was used as an instrument to carry out political objects, all has been confusion—the admixture of pagan worship, in which the mildness, charity, simplicity, and beauty of primitive Christianity were wholly lost. The sun of that faith, as I have already said, only rose at the period of the reformation, and has gone on gradually shedding its mild rays over the whole world. It only rose for us, for since that period we have enjoyed comparative tranquillity. But free by law, we are not so by

F

public opinion.. Prejudice still scowls upon us, denying us that estimation, that influence, that portion of worldly honours and rights which should appertain to the good citizen of every faith. We are not yet fully incorporated in the family of mankind. Christians by profession are not all Christians in practice; they have assumed to themselves the right to proscribe, the right to denounce, the right to punish, the right to hate, the right to judge, the right to condemn: and the afflictions under which the chosen people have suffered, from an assumption of these rights, have entailed an awful responsibility upon Christians. "Vengeance belongeth to me," saith the Lord; but it has been wrested from him by man. Where is the warrant for this persecution of the Jews—this innate feeling of hostility and prejudice against them—on the part of Christians? Not in the gentle spirit and forgiving kindness of their great Master. His example was more benign, his practice more charitable. He forgave the Jews with all his heart for any wrongs done to him; he prayed for them, loved them, and declared that he died for them; and yet those who profess to walk in his meek and lowly steps refuse to feel as he felt, to forgive as he forgave, and to love the children for the Father's sake. We have lost all—country, government, kingdom, and power. You have it all—it is yours. It was once ours—it is again to be restored to us. Dismiss, therefore, from your hearts all prejudice which still lurks there against the favoured people of God, and consider their miraculous preservation as a light and beacon for the great events which are to follow. They are worthy of your love, your confidence, and respect. Is it nothing to have had such fathers and founders of their faith as Abraham, Isaac, and Jacob; such mothers as Sarah and Rebecca, Leah and Rachel; such illustrious women as Miriam and Deborah, Ruth and Esther? Is it nothing to have been deemed worthy by the Almighty to have had a path made for them through the waste of waters; to have been led to Sinai, and there received the precious and Divine gift of that law which we all revere and hold sacred at this day? Is it nothing to have erected the Temple of Jerusalem, where the priesthood and Levites presented their votive and expiatory offerings to the Most High? Is it nothing, my friends, to have outlived all the nations of the earth, and to have survived all who sought to ruin and destroy us? Where are those who fought at Marathon, Salamis, and Platea? Where are the generals of Alexander—the mighty myriads of Xerxes? Where are the bones of those which once whitened the plains of Troy? We only hear of them in the pages of history. But if you ask, Where are the descendants of the million of brave souls who fell under the triple walls of Jerusalem? where are the subjects of David, and Solomon, and the brethren of Jesus? I answer, Here! Here we are—miraculously preserved—the pure and unmixed blood of the Hebrews, having the Law for our light, and God for our Redeemer.

How we have suffered, my friends, for steadily adhering to a belief in his unity, I need not pain you by recapitulating. Even to this day persecution has not sheathed its bloody sword. But if the Jews for eighteen hundred years have been assailed by the sword, by the rack, and the Inquisition, their great, and abiding, and absorbing faith has sustained them in the midst of those trials. When bound to the stake by men who claimed to be Christians, and the flames hissed and cracked around them; when, exhausted and dying, they called upon God to sustain them in their extremity, a still, small voice, pure and angelic, whispered in their ear, "Fear not, Jacob, for I am with thee."

Countrymen and citizens, thank God, your hands and hearts are free from the stains of such iniquity. If you have wronged Israel, it has arisen only from the prejudices of early education. Dismiss such feelings; be better acquainted with the Jew, and learn to estimate his virtues. See him in the bosom of his family, the best of fathers, and the truest of friends. See children dutiful, affectionate, and devotedly attached, supporting their parents with pride and exultation. See wives the most faithful, mothers the most devoted. Go with me into the haunts of misery, where the daughters of misfortune walk the streets of this great city, and see if among them all you find *one* Jewess. Come with me to the prisons, where crime riots and vice abounds, and examine whether a Jew is the tenant of a dungeon. Go into your almshouses, and ascertain how many Jews are recipients of your bounty. See them all, the friends of virtue and of temperance, obedient to the laws, and devoted to the country that protects them. Are we not, then, worthy of your confidence and esteem, discharging, as we do, every moral obligation imposed upon us? Vice and misfortune belong exclusively to no sect. Human nature is frail and fallible, and we should temper all our prejudices with mercy and charity.

Call to mind, therefore, whenever a feeling of prejudice is found lurking about your hearts against the chosen people, how much the world is indebted to the Jews. When you read the sublime Mosaic records, and see in them the wisdom and providence, the power and forgiving kindness, the confidence and affection of the Almighty, call to mind that Moses was a Jew. Whenever you pour out your hearts in devotion with the inspired Psalmist, and your whole soul is rapt in delight and devotion in dwelling upon his divine muse, remember also that *David* was a Jew. Whenever that mighty prophet, whose poetic soul was warmed by an ethereal fire, and who bears you on the wings of hope and exultation, of joy and rapture, remember that Isaiah was a Jew. But do not confine yourselves to the great army of kings and prophets of the Bible. Go to your own New Testament, and ask whether the Gentiles have *ever* had such evangelists as Judah furnished; and yet Paul, the mighty man of mind, of faith, and fervour, was a *Jew*—" a Hebrew of Hebrews."

And John, too, the gentle, the loving, and beloved, was likewise a Jew; but there is yet another, on whom all your affections are centred, to whom all your hopes and aspirations are directed, to whom you look for grace, and mercy, and salvation—Jesus of Nazareth was a Jew. and told you, in language which should sink deep into your hearts, as a commanding, imperative, and unrepealed precept and admonition, " Verily, I say unto you, inasmuch as ye have done those charities unto one of the *least* of these my brethren, ye have done it unto me."

I have referred to this country as the most suitable spot, from its character and institutions, from which a project of this kind might with security and success be undertaken, but has it ever occurred to you, my friends, that the eighteenth chapter of Isaiah might possibly have reference to America in connexion with the restoration of the Jews? Indulge me a moment in examining that short but singular chapter.

"Ho to the land" (it is translated *wo*, but evidently erroneously: it is *Ho*, or *Hail*)—" Hail to the land, shadowing with wings, which is beyond the rivers of Ethiopia."

The prophet, in this vision, was in Palestine, having Europe on his right, Africa on his left, and in front the Mediterranean Sea, and on looking down on the northern coast of Africa, speaks of a land "which is beyond the rivers of Ethiopia." That land is America; there is no other land which lies beyond the rivers of Cush known as Africa. But all lands spoken of in the Bible have a distinctive name; how is it that the Prophet Isaiah only speaks of it as "a land?" It was not discovered at the period of the prophecy, and, consequently, could have no name: it is our western world, and can mean no other. "Hail to the land, shadowing with wings." The arms of no country are so emphatically "wings" as those of the United States. It is an eagle in the act of flying with outspread wings, peculiarly conspicuous as an armorial ensign and living description of our land, which, under the shadow of her wings, offers a shelter for the persecuted of all nations. "That sendeth ambassadors by sea." This country cannot send ambassadors but by sea. On all the other continents they can be sent by land, "*even in vessels of bulrushes.*" Here "vessels," not ships, is the term used by the prophet. The true translation is, in vessels "impressing on the face of the water," answering to our steamboats; for the Hebrew word *gomey* is translated bulrushes: it is so, but it has two other meanings: one is, a rush of waters; the second is, *impresseth*, which is translated *yegomey*, meaning an impetus, a forcible propelling power; the third meaning is, the weed bulrush, which grows in the water; and, by-the-way, it may also be mentioned that our live oak is cut by men in water and among the bulrushes. These swift messengers, therefore, to carry ambassadors, may be construed into steam vessels. Here, then, we have the explanation of that verse. The land lying beyond the rivers of Ethiopia is America; the shadowing with wings is the American ensign, the emblem of its protective influence; "which sendeth ambassadors by sea," denotes the only country that must send those messengers on the ocean; and the vessels of bulrushes either applies to the light, fast-sailing vessels peculiar to our country, or our steam vessels. Thus far, I think, our country is fully indicated and shadowed forth in the vision of the prophet: "Go, ye swift messengers, to a nation scattered and peeled." This nation, it cannot be doubted, is the Jewish nation; "to a nation" means evidently "from a nation terrible from their beginning." It will be asked, In what respect have the Americans been "terrible from the beginning?" The most remarkably so of all the nations of the earth.

The Americans were not known for several hundred years, and their population, character, and resources, gradually developed, as other nations have been known, they sprang into immediate political existence from a state of vassalage to a condition of freemen; they were terrible to the foes of liberty, terrible to the kings and potentates of the world, terrible to the enemies of a republican form of government, terrible to their foes in war, terrible by their example to the despots of the earth, terrible, therefore, "from the beginning," because we may say we are but yet in the beginning, being only in the 68th year of American Independence. I ought, however, to say, that the word terrible means also "wonderful," which is equally applicable. The prophet, after saying that the Lord would take his rest, meaning that he would wait the issue of things in relation to the chosen people, abide his time, but still keep them as a dew in harvest, then comes to the concluding verse of this remarkable vision: "In that time shall the present be brought unto the Lord of hosts, a people scattered and peeled, and *from* a people terrible from their beginning hitherto; a nation meted out and trodden under foot, whose land the rivers have spoiled, to the place of the name of the Lord of hosts, the Mount Zion." For an explanation of what is meant by "whose land the rivers have spoiled," if you refer to the 8th chapter of Isaiah, the 7th and 8th verses, you will discover that rivers means conquerors rushing over and despoiling their land—a frequent occurrence in Judea

If I am right in this interpretation, and that this is the land which is beyond the rivers of Ethiopia, what a glorious privilege is reserved for the free people of the United States: the only country which has given civil and religious rights to the Jews equal with all other sects; the only country which has not persecuted them, selected and pointedly distinguished in prophecy as *the* nation which, at a proper time, shall present to the Lord his chosen and trodden-down people, and pave the way for their restoration to Zion. But will they go, I am asked, when the day of redemption arrives? All will go who feel the oppressor's yoke. *We* may repose where we are free and happy, but those who, bowed to the earth by oppression, would gladly exchange a condition of vassalage for the hope of freedom: that hope the Jews never can surrender; they cannot stand up against the prediction of our prophets, against the promises of God; they cease to be a nation, a people, a sect, when they do so. Either the Messiah of the Jews has come, or he is yet to come. If he has come, we must cease praying for him to come; if he has not come, we are bound to seek him, not here, but in our own land, which has been given to us as a perpetual inheritance, and which we dare not surrender without at once surrendering our faith. We must not stop to ask whether the Jews will consent to occupy the land of Israel as freemen. Restoration is not for us alone, but for millions unborn. There is no fanaticism in it; it is easy, tranquil, natural, and gradual. Let the people go: point out the path for them in safety, and they will go, not all, but sufficient to constitute the elements of a powerful government; and those who are happy here may cast their eyes towards the sun as it rises, and know that it rises on a free and happy people beyond the mountains of Judea, and feel doubly happy in the conviction that God has redeemed all his promises to Jacob. Who can be an infidel when he looks on the Jews, and sees in them, and the Bible yet firmly in their grasp, the consummation of all the Divine promises made to them as a nation? I should think that the very idea, the hope, the prospect, and, above all, the certainty of restoring Israel to his own and promised land, would arouse the whole civilized world to a cordial and happy co-operation. Mankind would spring from the couch of ease and slumber to see the ensign displayed, and would exclaim, " The day has come! the promise is fulfilled!"

Let me therefore impress upon your minds the important fact, that the liberty and independence of the Jewish nation may grow out of a single effort which this country may make in their behalf. That effort is to procure for them a permission to purchase and hold land in security and peace; their titles and possessions confirmed; their fields and flocks undisturbed. They want only PROTECTION, and the work is accomplished. The Turkish governments cannot be insensible to the fact that clouds are gathering around them, and destiny, in which they wholly confide, teaches them to await the day of trouble and dismemberment. It is their interest to draw around them the friendly aid and co-operation of the Jewish people throughout the world, by conferring these reasonable and just privileges upon them, and when Christianity exerts its powerful agency, and stretches forth its friendly hand, the rights solicited will be cheerfully conferred. When the Jewish people can return to Palestine, and feel that in their persons and property they are as safe from danger as they are under Christian governments, they will make their purchases of select positions, and occupy them peaceably and prosperously; confidence will then take the place of distrust and, by degrees, the population in every part of Syria being greatly increased, will become consolidated, and ready to unfold the standard when political events shall demonstrate to them that the time has arrived.

Let it, however, be kept in mind, that the restoration will be at first limited and partial; the government which they may form will be transitory and contingent; the great war prophesied in Ezekiel against Gog, prince of Rush, Meshech, and Tubal, the power which now controls *Archenaz*, *Refath*, and *Togarmah* of the Scriptures, that is to say, the Germans, Sclavonians, Sarmatians, and Turks of our day, is RUSSIA; the descendants of the joint colony of Meshech and Tubal, and the little horn of Daniel. Russia, in its attempt to wrest India from England and Turkey from the Ottomites, will make the Holy Land the theatre of a terrible conflict. TARSHISH, " with the young lions thereof"—evidently Great Britain, with her allies—will come to the rescue. Then will ensue the battle so sublimely described by the prophet: the fire and hailstones; the purification and victory; the advent of the Messiah, and the thousand years of happiness and peace which are to ensue.

Worldly as we may seem, and recurring to events which will grow out of the political destinies of Europe, we must still remember the overruling hand of Providence in the direction of these great results. What he has predicted has literally come to pass; what remains to be fulfilled will assuredly as literally *be* fulfilled. Skepticism and infidelity fade before the pure light of prophecy, prediction, and Divine assurance contained in the good Book, that book of life, and love, and hope, and promise, which some are weak enough to reject and repudiate. Remember, therefore, my countrymen, you whose aid is invoked to assist in the restoration, that we are to return as we went forth; to bring back to Zion the faith we carried away with us. The temple under Solomon, which we built as Jews, we must again erect as the chosen people. You believe that the Messiah has come; you are right in believing so; you have the evidences in the power and dominion, the wealth, the happiness, the glory that surrounds you. He has come for you, but how for us? We are still the peeled, banished, scattered, and oppressed people; the oil on the surface of the ocean, which mingles not with the heaving billows. For us he is yet to come, and will come. For two thousand years we have been pursued and persecuted, and we are yet here; assemblages of men have formed communities, built cities, established governments, rose, prospered, decayed, and fell, and yet *we* are here. Rome conquered Greece, and she was no longer Greece. Rome, in turn, became conquered, and there are but few traces now of the once mistress of the world; yet we are still here, like the fabled Phœnix, ever springing from its ashes, or, more beautifully typical, like the bush of Moses, which ever burns, yet never consumes. You believe that Jesus of Nazareth was the Messiah, and you are Christians; were we to believe the same, we should still be Jews.

With this difference only, what is it that separates the Jew and the Gentile? Our law is your law, our prophets are your prophets, our hope is your hope, our salvation is your salvation, our God is your God. Why should we change? Why surrender that staff of Jacob which has guided our steps through so many difficulties? We can never be separated from our Shepherd; we believe in all that he has promised, and patiently await their fulfilment. Come, therefore, to our aid, and take the lead in this great work of restoration. Let the first movement for the emancipation of the Jewish nation come from this free and liberal country. Call to mind that Moses was the first founder of a republican form of government, and that the first settlers on this continent adopted the Mosaic laws as their code, and strictly enforced them.

In the appeal I have made to my fellow-citizens this evening, let it not be supposed that I mean to exclude from a participation in the great and good work, the beloved friend and companion of man; second in creation, but first in zeal and true religion. Their agency is ever of the highest importance in good works. When surrounded by the excitements of the busy world, intent on gain, and eager in the pursuit of fortune, when the mind is wholly engrossed in temporal objects, then, in the watches of the night and the stillness of the morn, the wife awakens the husband to a sense of religious delinquency, and calm admonition gradually but imperceptibly leads him into the path of duty and high moral obligations. Like the woman in the evangelists, who freely and happily used her box of precious ointment, all that she says and urges in the fulfilment of the most sacred duties drops like oily balsam upon the heart, soothes while it influences, and subdues while it controls. Jew or Gentile, women are ever the pillars of the Church.

And now, with the most grateful acknowledgments for the liberal attention you have honoured me with this evening, I do commend you all to the gracious protection of that Divine Providence in whom we all hope, who is all love, all mercy, and all mighty.

ZIONISM in PROPHECY

THE RETURN OF ISRAEL TO THE HOLY LAND

A Fulfilment of Biblical Promises

with Introductory Chapters by
CHARLES EDWARD RUSSELL
and
DR. HIRSCH LOEB GORDON

(Copyright 1936)

Distributed by
PRO-PALESTINE FEDERATION OF AMERICA
307 Fifth Avenue, New York, N. Y.

Printed in U. S. A.

INTRODUCTION

Two eminent scholars and writers—the one a Gentile, the other a Jew—were asked to critically study this booklet before publication, then briefly set forth their conclusions. Charles Edward Russell certainly needs no introduction.—See "Who's Who in America." The other reviewer was Dr. Hirsch Loeb Gordon, the well known Jewish writer, Hebraic scholar and Talmudist, who holds degrees from Yale, Columbia, Jewish Theological Seminary, Catholic University of America, and the University of Rome. The Pro-Palestine Federation of America is glad to be able to present these sympathetic forewords by two outstanding men of letters:

Charles Edward Russell writes:

IN THE midst of the night of gloom that settled upon the world after 1929, one spot remained that glowed with light and resounded with human activities.

In Jewish Palestine there was no unemployment, but a demand for labor beyond the supply. In Jewish Palestine there was no want, no bread lines, no relief work at public expense; but, with the joyful impetus of a new hope, men were redeeming a wilderness. In but a little more than a decade of effort a transformation had been wrought that seemed almost magical.

We have been accustomed to assume that when men put forth their great efforts, undergo severe hardships, battle valiantly with the forces of nature, practice self-denials, their one purpose is eventual personal aggrandizement. Here was an instance where an impulse much stronger than profits led men and women to vast labors upon a deliberated plan of betterment, wiser, more enlightened, more pertinent to human welfare and happiness than had ever before been known.

A circle of thoughtful men watched, applauded a

little, and wondered more. To build a state upon the basis of atonement for centuries of hideous wrong—with principles of justice, freedom, safeguarded opportunity for all—here was something so new in human history and experience that it seemed unreal or unattainable. This novel method of state-building in Palestine involved no marching armies, no battling of hosts, no devastation and horror, but only peaceable purchase and friendly development. If it succeeds, it should strike the soul of imperialism into shame-faced retreat.

That such an innovation in state-building should come from the Jews, to whom the world is already indebted for so many civilizing influences, seems singularly apt and appropriate. The Jews throughout the centuries have been consistent opponents of the insanity of war, the steadfast champions of even-handed justice.

In the succeeding pages the author has set forth, convincingly and accurately, the remarkable achievements in this peaceful transformation of Palestine by the Zionists. What he has written deserves to be noted and remembered for its careful additions to the sum of general knowledge concerning this significant peaceful revolution.

But he has gone further; he has gathered for us the very sources of the immeasurable spiritual inspiration that has made possible this greatly memorable excursion. He has assembled from the revered Jewish prophets the ancient forecasts of this Jewish vindication which has begun so promisingly in the Palestine of today.

His handling of these prophecies shows this author to be a profound Biblical scholar, and equally profound in his understanding of and sympathy for the people who have suffered such vast historic injustice. The reading of these prophecies will startle into keen interest all reflective minds, some of whom perhaps may here come upon such an array of forecastings for the first time.

The number of prophecies that already have come

true, and the number that now seem on the eve of fulfilment, assail skepticism and justify the query whether this people who, through dispersion, persecution and tyranny at the hands of majorities which they have suffered so long and so patiently, have not been justified in their unshaken faith in the beneficence and infinite support of the Divine Power.

We all are indebted to the author for his lucid treatment of both phases of the Palestine question in this admirable little book. He has made the Biblical prophecies clear and the Jewish achievements in Palestine luminous.

CHARLES EDWARD RUSSELL

Dr. Hirsch Loeb Gordon writes:

IN addition to those great prophets of Israel who were chosen mouthpieces of Jehova, there also were some ancient Gentile sages with prophetic vision, among whom was Balaam, also the faithful Job.

Now, after a lapse of thirty-three centuries, there arises another Gentile—one to expound the prophets, and to encourage the tribes of Israel in their present fervent quest for the holy land.

The author here pleads Israel's cause before the bar of world opinion. In this booklet, "Zionism in Prophecy," he vividly recalls the many divine assurances made to this people, that they would be regathered to the land from which they were plucked, and then shows that the present day Zionist movement for the rehabilitation of our homeland is in fulfilment of those Biblical promises.

"Gentile prophets," said one of our ancient sages, "see their visions in the darkness of the night." Certainly this Gentile voice from America is now being raised in the midst of darkness—at a time when beastly persecutions are being heaped upon Jewry in various parts of the world.

In his affectionate approach to this Jewish agony of

the present time, our author wisely abstains from justifying it in the name of misunderstood Biblical admonitions. He sees Israel as "a scattered, homeless and oft persecuted people ... distinct and homogenous ... bound together by suffering and oft-deferred hopes"—a people that cannot regain their former spiritual heights while in diaspora.

Any true believer in the inspired Scriptures, whether he be Jew or Gentile, cannot fail to become enthused by this author's scholarly proofs that the divinely "set time" for Jacob's final return to his homeland coincides with the events of today—all pointing to the fulfilment of the covenant made by God to Abraham (Gen. 15:18), to the termination of the era of "seven times" of chastisement foretold by Moses (Lev. 26), to the culmination of the four World Empires shown to Nebuchadnezzar in the dream that troubled his spirit, and to the fulfilment of the prophetic writing upon the wall of Belshazzar's palace when he made a great feast to a thousand of his lords.

The discouraged Jew will find in this author's interpretation of the prophecies emboldment, reassurance, confirmation of his millennial hope of rebuilding the ruins of Jerusalem, replanting the arid fields of Judah, and relighting on Mt. Moriah the glorious and everlasting torch of peace and truth.

The Gentile reader will find herein the conviction that in helping the Jew, his fellowman, to reestablish his home in the holy land, he thereby becomes an instrument in God's hand for speeding the realization of the divine promises.

Everyone, Jew and Gentile, should wish this valiant author, in whose unusual thesis deep scholarship and true religion vie with each other, shall have the greatest success in his noble mission, and that of him it may be said, in the words of that great Gentile prophet of old: "Unto me men gave ear and waited. . . . After my words they spoke not in indifference. . . . They opened their mouth wide as for the latter rain."—Job 29:22, 23.

HIRSCH LOEB GORDON

Zionism in Prophecy

"Thou shalt arise and have mercy upon Zion; for the time to favor her, yea, the set time, is come."
—Psalm 102:13.

THE modern Zionist movement, which began as a dream in the mind of Theodor Herzl and started to take definite form as an organized Jewish effort over forty years ago, is now a permanently established entity and a compelling force in the life of Jewry the world over. Even non-Jewish statesmen of many countries are equally interested with Israel in this national Zionist movement, which is now being selfishly opposed by great Arab land owners and paid agitators.

Today the need for a Jewish National Home is more acutely recognized than ever before; by reason of the fact that within the past few years more than 300,000 Jews have been forced to flee from Germany, Poland, Russia and elsewhere and take again the wanderer's staff, or seek a definite haven in lands overseas. More than half of these emigrants have already found their way to Palestine.

There are countless reasons why Israel should be interested in Palestine as a Jewish Homeland. The economic advantages of such an undertaking have been stressed, and these properly constitute a great attraction to pioneers. A latent nationalistic pride or patriotism has actuated others. Purely sentimental reasons have constituted the primary incentive for many. Persecutions have literally driven others there in spite of themselves. And faith in the predictions of the ancient prophets, and in the hitherto unfulfilled promises of God to His chosen people, has been a stimulus and a compelling force in not a few instances. All these reasons are substantial; but perhaps the one of greatest importance, and yet the one heretofore least emphasized and appreciated, is the religious reason last mentioned.

The purpose of this discussion, therefore, is to direct anew the attention of Jewry to various prophecies of the Sacred Scriptures which undoubtedly are being fulfilled today in the National Zionist Movement. These prophecies indicate that it is God's purpose that the faithful of Israel shall again be regathered to this ancient holy land, and there eventually become the nucleus of an important nation which shall exert a mighty force for good in all the world; and shall literally fulfil, on a hitherto unprecedented scale, the original oath-bound promise to the patriarch Abraham, "In thy seed shall all nations be blessed."

It cannot be denied that the prophets do foretell an ultimate regathering of Israel to their homeland. It was the prophet Jeremiah who declared: "I will bring them again to this land [Palestine]; and I will build them, and *not pull them down;* and I will plant them, and *not pluck them up.* And I will give them a heart to know Me, that I am the Lord; and they shall be My people, and I will be their God; for they shall return unto Me with their whole heart." —Jeremiah 24: 5-7.

It cannot be said that the return of Jewry from their seventy years' captivity to Babylon fulfilled this prophecy; for after that return they were again pulled down and repeatedly plucked up; whereas the prophet here predicted a time to come wherein they would never again be plucked up from their ancient homeland. Since Jeremiah was a true prophet of God, and his various other predictions were fulfilled, there is no reason to doubt that this prediction also shall be fulfilled eventually; and later on in this narrative we will present evidence to indicate that the time for its fulfilment is at hand.

The same prophet also foretold the future dispersion of the Jews into all the earth, and even indicated the fact that they would mainly go to lands north of Palestine—such as Russia, Poland, etc. Then he foretold their ultimate return to their homeland, in these encouraging words:

"Behold, I will bring them from the north country, and gather them from the coasts of the earth. . . . A great company shall return thither. They shall come with weeping; and with supplications shall I lead them. . . . Hear the word of the Lord, O ye nations, and declare it in the isles afar off, and say, 'He that scattered Israel will gather him, and keep him as a shepherd doth his flock; for the Lord hath redeemed Jacob and ransomed him from the hand of him that was stronger that he.' Therefore, they shall come and sing in the height of Zion . . . and they shall not sorrow *any more at all*."—Jer. 30: 18-21; 31: 8-12.

Again the prophet declared: "Behold, the days come, saith the Lord, that it shall no more be said, 'The Lord liveth, that brought up the children of Israel out of the land of Egypt'; but, 'The Lord liveth, that brought up the children of Israel from the land of the north, and from all the lands whither He had driven them': and I will bring them again into their land that I gave unto their fathers. Behold, I will send for many *fishers,* saith the Lord, and they shall fish them: and after will I send for many *hunters,* and they shall hunt them."—Jer. 16: 14-16.

The reference here to "fishers" and to "hunters," as a means to "bring them again into their land," seems significant. A fisher uses bait to *attract* the fish; whereas a hunter usually fights and kills, or *drives out,* his prey. And both these means are being utilized today in the regathering and rebuilding of the Jewish National Home. The Zionist agencies have been exerting an attractive force for four decades, as a result of which a large aggregation of

Jews from all parts of the world have been regathered. But what the "fisher" method has failed to do, the "hunter" method is now accomplishing—yea, the heavy hand of the persecutor recently has been raised against Jewry in many pestilential spots of Europe, as a result of which thousands of refugees have had to flee, and are finding their way to Palestine. Thus are the prophet's words finding literal fulfilment in this our day.

The prophet Ezekiel likewise predicted: "And I shall place you in your own land: then shall ye know that I the Lord have spoken it, and performed it, saith the Lord." (Ezek. 37:14.) In similar vein did the prophet Amos declare:

"In that day will I raise up the tabernacle of David that is fallen, and close up the breaches thereof; and I will raise up his ruins, and I will build it as in days of old. And I will bring again the captivity of My people Israel, and they shall build the waste cities and inhabit them; and they shall plant vineyards and drink the wine thereof; they shall also make gardens, and eat the fruit of them. And I will plant them upon their land, and they shall *no more be pulled up* out of their land which I have given them, saith the Lord God."—Amos 9:11-15.

Such prophecies as these cannot be logically interpreted in any symbolic sense. It is not a Canaan in heaven that is referred to, but a Canaan on earth. Israel is to be planted again "upon their own land," the land of their fathers, which God had given them; the land which was divinely promised to Abraham and his seed as an "everlasting possession." The promise is from God Himself, and must be fulfilled eventually. That original promise to Abraham reads:

"Lift up now thine eyes and look from the place where thou art, northward, and southward, and eastward, and westward: for all the land which thou seest, to thee will I give it, and to thy seed *forever*. . . . Arise, walk through the land, in the length of it, and in the breadth of it; for I will give it unto thee. . . . I will give it unto thee, and to thy seed after thee, the land wherein thou art a stranger, all the land of Canaan, for an *everlasting possession.*"—Genesis 13:14-17; 17:8.

His Promises Are Sure

Long has Israel awaited the fulfilment of these ancient promises—even for the time when they would be permanently established in the land that was given them, never again to be plucked up. A scattered, homeless and oft persecuted people, they are still a distinct and homogeneous people. United by ties of blood, by common characteristics, manners, customs and religion, with common hopes inspired by a common faith in the utterances of their ancient prophets and in the sure promises of the one true God (though they may have but dimly comprehended the full significance of many of those divine promises), and still further bound together by a bond of sympathy growing out of their common sufferings and privations as exiles, the faithful of Israel to this day look and long for the fruition of their oft-deferred hopes. They realize that God, in His wisdom, has a definite time for the accomplishment of each feature of His great plan for His chosen people, and for all mankind; even as the inspired Psalmist declared:

"Thou shalt arise and have mercy upon Zion; for the time to favor her, yea, the *set* time, is come. For Thy servants take pleasure in her stones, and favor the dust thereof. Then shall the Gentiles fear (reverence) the name of Jehovah, and all the kings of the earth thy glory. When the Lord shall build up Zion, He shall appear in His glory."—Psalms of David, 102:13-18.

It must be admitted that many in Jewry today have lost faith in the inspiration of the Sacred Scriptures as the Word of God; and now look upon the Hebrew prophecies as a mere collection of "wise sayings" of ancient philosophers which have no particular significance for our day. Perhaps this generation of moderns should not be unduly blamed for their skeptical attitude toward the Scriptures, in view of the fact that the world has been flooded of late with literature in criticism of the sacred writings. But an earnest study of the Law and the Prophets, apart from the traditions and theories of men, should convince any sincere seeker for truth that there exists in His heaven a personal, intelligent Creator; One who is superior to the things that have been created; One who is orderly in His dealings in behalf of humanity, and most definite in His shaping of the destiny of His people Israel.

The prophetic Psalm above quoted mentions a time, a "set time," for the return of divine favor to Zion. And this same principle of orderliness is exemplified in all God's arrangements, as described throughout the sacred Scriptures. God timed the entrance of Abraham into Canaan, and the migration of Jacob into Egypt; also the rise of Moses, the Exodus, the wandering in the wilderness, the conquest of Canaan, and eventually the establishment of the Jewish kingdom. In due time David, Solomon and other monarchs appeared; and each of them represented God Himself in the theocratic kingdom of Israel, and later of Judah. It was said that they "sat upon the throne of the kingdom of the Lord."—1 Chron. 28:5.

Overturned "Until He Come"

Eventually, and at a "set time," the sceptre was taken from Zedekiah, the last king of Judah, "until He shall come whose right it is"; as had been foretold by the prophet Ezekiel. (Ezek. 21:17.) When dominion was thus taken from King Zedekiah, at the time of Jerusalem's destruction by the Babylonians, the Gentiles began their long domination of the Jewish homeland, which has continued on down to this day. This has been by divine permission and for a divine purpose. But such domination is not to continue forever; for God has a time, yea, a "set time," to return His favor to Zion, and to plant her again in her own land, never again to be plucked up.

The God of Israel has recognized these dominating Gentile powers, for a purpose; but not in the sense that He had recognized His own chosen people. He called Nebuchadnezzar, the Babylonian monarch, "My servant"; for he served the divine purpose of visiting punishment upon Judah, "because ye have not heard My words." (Jer. 25:8, 9.) But neither Babylon nor any other Gentile power has ever been designated "the kingdom of the Lord," as was said of those of the Davidic line. (2 Chron. 13:8.) Nor was any Gentile dynasty ever assured perpetuity of rule, as was promised to the offspring of David.—2 Sam. 7:16, 17; Isa. 11.

The Gentile powers were merely granted a "lease" over the holy land for a definite term, as a punishment for Israel's and Judah's idolatries and unfaithfulness. Then, at the time appointed, this Gentile lease of power was to terminate; and forthwith He would "assemble the outcasts of Israel, and gather together the dispersed of Judah from the four corners of the earth." (Isa. 11:12.) Then God's original purposes for all Israel would be resumed, she would be established in her homeland, and once more her opportunity to represent Him in the earth would return to her, exactly as the ancient prophets of Israel had foretold. Is it possible then that this modern Zionist movement is not merely the creature of Herzl's or of Israel's natural longings, but has come about in this our day by divine providence, simply because "the time to favor her, yea, the *set time,* is come," as predicted in the foregoing prophetic Psalm? We believe the evidence, as set forth in the following pages, actually justifies that conclusion.

Gentile Dominion Foreseen in Vision

Ezekiel tells us that Zedekiah, Judah's last king, was both profane and wicked, and that the time had come when such iniquity should have an end. Hence the crown was removed, the Jewish kingdom was overturned; and the homeland was to remain under Gentile domination "until He come whose right it is, and I will give it unto Him." (Ezek. 21:25-27.) This One who was to come is the great Messiah, who is to be a Branch out of Jesse and of David (Isa. 11:1-4), and whose Kingdom is to be an everlasting and righteous dominion. At the time of Zedekiah's overthrow, therefore, a parenthesis was divinely declared in the Davidic rule; and Gentiles were given a lease of power over Jerusalem during this interim. All this was prophetically seen and foretold; not only by Ezekiel, but specifically by the prophet Daniel—when he interpreted King Nebuchadnezzar's remarkable dream or vision.—Daniel 2:25-47.

This vision which the king of Babylon saw was no ordinary dream; it was divinely implanted in his mind, and also the interpretation of it in the mind of Daniel. God simply took this means of revealing to His chosen people in advance the fact that successive Gentile world-powers would be permitted to dominate the holy land throughout the coming centuries, until the "set time" shall come when He shall have mercy upon Zion and return to her His favor. The vision which the king saw in his dream was that of a stupendous image or statue, with a head made of gold, breast and arms of silver, belly and thighs of brass, legs of iron, and feet of iron intermingled with clay. Then a stone smote the image and broke it to pieces. Then the stone grew and filled the earth.

When none of Nebuchadnezzar's counsellors or wise men could interpret this vision, the captain of the king's guard "brought in Daniel before the king in haste, and said thus unto him, 'I have found a man of the captives of Judah, that will make known unto the king the interpretation.' . . . Daniel answered in the presence of the king, and said, . . . 'There is a God in heaven that revealeth secrets, and maketh known to the king Nebuchadnezzar what shall be in the latter days."—Dan. 2:25-28.

Four World Empires

Daniel then explained that this image pictured earthly dominion, and that Nebuchadnezzar's kingdom was represented by the head of gold. "And after thee shall arise another kingdom, inferior to thee; and another third kingdom of brass, which shall bear rule over all the earth. And the fourth kingdom shall be strong as iron: forasmuch as iron breaketh in pieces and subdueth all things. . . . And whereas thou sawest the feet and toes, part of potter's clay and part of iron, the kingdom shall be divided; but there shall be in it of the strength of iron. . . . And as the toes of the feet were part of iron and part of clay, so the kingdom shall be partly strong and partly brittle . . . they shall mingle themselves with the seed of men, but they shall not cleave one to another. . . . And in the days of these kings [represented in the toes] shall the God of heaven set up a Kingdom, which shall never be destroyed . . . It shall break in pieces and consume all these kingdoms; and it shall stand forever; forasmuch as thou sawest that the stone was cut out of the mountain without hands, and that it break in pieces the iron, the brass, the clay, the silver and the gold. The great God hath made known to the king what shall come to pass hereafter: the dream is certain, and the interpretation thereof sure."— Dan. 2:36-45.

Even as this image was in four main parts—being made of gold, silver, brass and iron—so has history disclosed just four great world-empires, namely, Babylon, Medo-Persia, Greece and Rome. The two arms, united to the breast, all of silver, represented the Medes and the Persians as united under Cyrus, who conquered Babylon in 536-8 B. C. Then Greece, under Alexander, subdued and succeeded the Medo-Persians as world conqueror. Then came the strong power of Pagan Rome, represented by the two iron legs—with one foot planted at Byzantium on the Bosporus, and the other on the Tibur, in the West. These iron legs were firm and powerful; but later the Roman empire, in both the east and the west, ceased to be a strictly civil power and came to be dominated by church authority; and was then known as the *"Holy* Roman Empire." Eventually Byzantium, or Constantinople, became the head of the eastern Catholic communion, while Rome was the centre of western Papal authority. Thus were the iron feet of civil authority intermingled or smeared with the clay of ecclesiasticism, exactly as foretold by Daniel the prophet. Here also is seen the course of human history—beginning with gold, it terminates in nothing better than clay.

At the terminus of each foot of the image were subdivisions, representing the "toes." These, too, were mixed with clay, and thus were made to appear like stone—a counterfeit of the true "stone" kingdom of God, which eventually was to smite the image, demolish and supercede it. These toes clearly represent the ten original cleavages of the "Holy Roman Empire" which exist in Europe to this day, many of which have crumbled as "kingdoms" within the past few years and are now in a state of change. Thus we are now living in the final days of Gentile domination, as represented in the "toes" of this symbolic image. No other great Gentile empire is to arise in the earth. The next thing to expect is the true kingdom of God, represented by the little "stone," which is to grow until its beneficent influence becomes worldwide.

Each of the world empires represented in the image, as interpreted by Daniel, were to have definitely appointed limits—a fixed time for their beginning and an "appointed time" for their duration and termination. There were never to be any other empires than those here mentioned, to tread down Jerusalem and dominate Zion. The vision itself was of divine appointment, its interpretation was by divine wisdom, and therefore its fulfilment is sure—it can neither be annulled, obstructed nor checkmated by anything that men may do. Daniel also disclosed that the full understanding of these things would be revealed only at the "time of the end." (Dan. 12:4, 8, 9.) If therefore we can now understand the meaning of this vision, this is further proof that we have come to the "time of the end" of the Gentile lease of power, and are approaching the time when God "shall arise and have mercy upon Zion; for the time to favor her, yea, the *set* time, is come."

"I Will Chastise You Seven Times"

THE long period of national affliction that has been visited upon Jewry, had been foretold long before the Babylonian captivity and Zedekiah's overthrow. In Leviticus 26: 27, 28, the Lord spake to Israel through Moses, saying, "And if ye will not for all this hearken unto Me; then I will walk contrary unto you also in fury; and I, even I, will chastise you *seven times* for your sins." This warning of "seven times" of punishment was repeated four times in this same chapter, and is also alluded to elsewhere in the Scriptures. This word "times" (Hebrew *paam*) literally means to strike or chastise with regular blows or strokes. It therefore may be used to signify *periodic divisions of time* during which chastisement or trouble is being endured. Hence this word in the singular is sometimes conventionally used to signify a *year* of trouble: and "seven times" would thus indicate "seven years" of affliction upon Zion.

But it is manifest that this supreme period of punishment could not refer to seven *literal* years; for Israel had been afflicted for much longer periods than that prior to the pronouncement of this prophecy. Moses referred to these prior punishments; and then said, "If ye will not for all this hearken" unto the Lord, then He will chastise you "seven times"—thus clearly indicating that the "seven times," or seven years, here prophecied, would be a much longer and greater punishment than Israel had ever been called upon to suffer in the past; greater even than their long enslavement in Egypt from which Moses had recently delivered them. Nor could the subsequent seventy-years captivity to Babylon have fulfilled this dire prediction of "seven times," for it was not as great a punishment as that endured back in the days of Egyptian bondage.

A Day for a Year

What, then, could these "seven times" refer to; and how long a period would they actually cover?

Perhaps a clue is given us in the prophecy of Ezekiel. This prophet wrote while in captivity at Babylon. He was divinely instructed in a vision to lie on his left side for 390 days, and then to turn and lie on his right side for 40 days more. This the prophet did, lying helplessly as if bound; while the other captives doubtless wondered what it all meant. But the Lord explained to the prophet, "I have laid upon thee the *years* of their iniquity, according to the number of *days,* three hundred and ninety days: so shalt thou bear the iniquity of the house of Israel. And when thou hast accomplished them, lie again on thy right side, and thou shalt bear the iniquity of the house of Judah forty days: I have appointed thee *each day for a year.*" (Ezek. 4:4-6.) Thus Ezekiel symbolized the 390 years exile of the ten-tribe kingdom to Assyria; and the remaining 40 years of captivity that Judah must yet endure before being released from Babylon.

In similar manner, may it not be that God intended that the "seven times," or seven years, of affliction mentioned in Leviticus 26:27, 28, also were to be fulfilled on the basis of a "day for a year"? This seems to be a logical conclusion since these "seven times" manifestly were to exceed in severity all other punishments that had been visited upon this chosen people. If therefore these "seven times" could not refer to seven *literal* years, they must mean seven *symbolic* years; that is, "each day for a year." A solar year, of course, contains a fraction over 365 days, but in computing "symbolic time" as it is set forth in the Scriptures, students of prophecy find that the writers simply divided the year into 12 months of 30 days each. In other words, a *time,* or year, in Scriptural symbology, refers to 360 solar years—each day representing a year. "Seven times," then, would signify 7 times 360, or 2520 years.

Duration of the Gentile Lease

Is it possible then that the Gentile "lease" of authority over Zion was to continue 2520 years, and that thereafter she would be permitted to repossess her rightful heritage? Let us see how this suggestion works out. The final treading down or domination of Jerusalem by Gentiles, from which there was no subsequent release, began when Nebuchadnezzar of Babylon came and subjugated the land and took his first Jewish captives. This was a few years before he actually dethroned Zedekiah, the last Jewish king, and destroyed Jerusalem. Some historians claim that the subjugation of Judah began in 606 B. C., while others claim that that date marks the actual destruction of Jerusalem. In any event, we may take this date as marking the practical beginning of the Gentile lease of power, and the start of Zion's national affliction.

Now if the "seven times," or 2520 years, of Gentile domination, and of national chastisement upon Zion, began about 606 B. C., when would that period end? Strangely enough, 2520 years after 606 B. C. brings us to the important date 1914 A. D. when the World War began; and out of that conflict came the ousting of the Turks from Jerusalem by General Allenby, the famous Balfour Declaration, the opening of the ancient homeland to Jewish refugees and pioneers from all lands, and the infusion of the whole Zionist movement with new life and hope. It would seem, then, that we are now at the termination of the "seven times" of national affliction upon Israel, and that the events that are now taking place in Palestine in behalf of Jewry are the early beginnings of a new day; that the long lease of power to the Gentiles is up, and that the dispossession of the old tenant and the repossession by the rightful owner is actually under way.

The Handwriting on the Wall

Another possible corroboration of the fact that the period of the Gentile lease of power would be 2520 years, seems to be contained in the "handwriting on the wall" which appeared at Belshazzar's feast on the night in which that co-regent son of Babylon's last king was killed and the empire overthrown by Cyrus the Medo-Persian conqueror. Daniel pointed the revelers to the words that flashed miraculously across the palace wall, and which read as follows: "Mene, Mene, Tekel, Upharsin." What could this strange message mean? Daniel told them that it signified, for one thing, that the Babylonish kingdom had been "weighed in the balances and found wanting"—these four words being Chaldaic units of weights and measures. Being translated literally from the ancient cuneiform in which they were written, they would read: "A mina, a mina, a shekel and a divided mina"—that is, a half-mina.

But why were these, and only these, particular symbols of Babylonish weights and measures used?

Was there any further or hidden meaning to them, than the general fact that the Babylonish empire had been weighed in the balances of God? It would seem so. A mina is 50 shekels, and a shekel is 20 gerahs; hence let us reduce this formula to gerahs and see what number it yields. One mina would be 1,000 gerahs; and "a mina, a mina, a shekel and a half-mina," or two and a half minas plus a shekel, when reduced to gerahs, yields the number 2520—exactly the same number that we have seen symbolized in the "seven times" of Israel's punishment at Gentile hands.

It would seem, therefore, that this message that God flashed to the leaders of Babylon, which was the first of the four great Gentile powers—the "head" of the image of Nebuchadnezzar's dream—not only signified that Babylon's days were numbered, but that the total days of Gentile supremacy were also numbered, and that the number is 2520 years. Counting this period from the year 606 B. C., we have noted that it terminated in 1914 A. D., and that in that very year the World War broke out, and events began to happen in rapid succession looking toward the reestablishment of Israel in her homeland, and the ushering in of a new order for all humanity. We are now at the end of the 2520 years of the Gentile lease of power over Jerusalem, and not only Jewry but the whole world is clearly experiencing some momentous transition—a new order is coming in. Every statesman realizes that fact.

This number 2520 is distinctive, in that it is the least common multiple of all the digits in our system of numbers. That is, it is the least possible number that can be divided by each of the digits, from 1 up to 10. Thus it is seen that, in this special sense, 2520 is an all-comprehensive number, and therefore is the best number to portray the total duration of such an important period as that of Gentile supremacy over the holy land. No other number could be so appropriate for spanning the whole period of this long lease of power to the Gentiles. And, at the same time, this number is exactly *seven* symbolic years in duration. Here, then is a further prophetic clue that we are now at the end of the old order, and that a new order of things is now gradually being ushered in—a new day for Israel and for mankind generally.

These things, of course, are not to be accomplished in a day. The lease has been long, and the full change of occupancy may require considerable time. Nor is it the wish of Zionists that other peoples who now live in the holy land should be summarily ousted or dealt with unfairly. Though Israel has long suffered injustices, she has no desire to visit injustices upon others. The transition, however, must go on apace, for God's time to favor Zion, "yea, the *set* time," has come. Jewish immigrants are being received into the Homeland as rapidly as present conditions will permit; and the entire country is taking on a new lease of life and throbbing with new activities under the hands of these zealous pioneers who recognize it to be their rightful inheritance.

Another Prophetic Clue

Another prophetic suggestion from which we may infer that now is the time for the seed of Abraham to inherit their land, seems to be contained in God's strange answer to Abraham, when the patriarch asked for a token whereby he may know that he shall inherit Canaan. The Scripture reads: "I am the Lord that brought thee out of Ur of the Chaldees, to give thee this land to inherit it. And he said, 'Lord God, whereby shall I know that I shall inherit it?' And He said unto him, 'Take Me an heifer of three years old, and a she goat of three years old, and a ram of three years old, and a turtle dove, and a young pigeon!"—Genesis 15:7-9.

This was a peculiar reply for God to give to the patriarch's query. What did it mean? It is difficult to see any meaning in it, unless it be that the ages of the animals He specified are significant. Three of the animals were to be 3 years old each. No age was mentioned for the young pigeon and the turtle dove, but if they were young they would be of the first year. If then we count 1 year for each of them and 3 years each for the other animals so designated, and add them together, we have a total of 11 years. Perhaps, then, God's cryptic answer to Abraham was that his seed would inherit the land for a lasting possession after 11 years. But He could not have meant 11 *literal* years. Might He not then have signified 11 *symbolic* years? That seems reasonable, especially when we work it out.

We have seen that a symbolic *month,* in Bible prophecy, refers to 30 years—each day representing a year—and that a symbolic *year* consists of 12 symbolic months, or 360 literal years. Hence 11 symbolic years would be 3960 literal years. And, strange as it may seem, it has been just about that length of time since God gave the foregoing peculiar reply to Abraham's straightforward inquiry concerning his future inheritance of Canaan. We cannot be sure as to the exact date when this conversation occurred, but the context in which the account is found shows that it took place shortly before the time when Abram's son Isaac was born. Bible chronologers compute Isaac's birth from about 2007 to 2026 B. C. If this be approximately correct, then 11 symbolic years, or 3960 literal years, from that time brings us right down here to the very days in which we now live, wherein we do see the repossession of this ancient homeland, as the rightful inheritance of Abraham's seed, actually taking place. Here again is another clue by which Israel may infer that Gentile domination of her ancient homeland is about ended, that the "lease" to the alien has expired, and that God's "set time" for a change of occupancy has come.

Daniel's Vision of the Four Beasts

In the seventh chapter of Daniel's prophecy is another description of that same long period of Gentile rule, which began with the Babylonian captivity. Daniel, who had been taken to Babylon among the early captives, was given a vision of those same four world-powers that were represented in the four parts of the great "image" which Nebuchadnezzar had seen in his dream and which Daniel interpreted. But in Daniel's own vision he saw these four powers in the form of four wild "beasts," ruthlessly trampling others under foot to gain their ends. The beastly character of Babylon, Medo-Persia, Greece, Rome, and the subdivisions of the latter, were amply displayed during their ascendancy—the rights of lesser peoples seldom, if ever, being taken into consideration whenever they ran counter to the ambitions or desires of those who wielded sufficient power. In every war the nations have torn at each other's throats like wild beasts, down to and including the World War, which saw the slaughter of five million of the flower of youth and the maiming of fifteen million more—in the name of civilization.

The "seven times" of the Gentiles are synchronous with the reign of these four beasts—the fourth of which "was diverse from all others, exceedingly dreadful, whose teeth were of iron, and his nails of brass; which devoured, break in pieces, and stamped the residue with his feet. . . . Thus he said, The fourth beast shall be the fourth kingdom [fourth world empire] upon earth, which shall be diverse from all kingdoms, and shall devour the whole earth, and shall tread it down and break it in pieces. And the ten horns out of this kingdom are ten kings that shall arise: and others shall rise after them. . . . But the judgment shall sit, and they shall take away his dominion, to consume and to destroy it unto the end. And the kingdom and dominion, and the greatness of the kingdom under the whole heaven, shall be given to the people of the saints of the Most High, whose kingdom is an everlasting kingdom, and all dominions shall serve and obey Him."—Dan. 7:19-27.

Note that in Nebuchadnezzar's dream, the image was in four parts, and the feet of the fourth part were divided into ten toes. In Daniel's vision of the four beasts, the fourth beast developed ten horns. There were just ten original subdivisions of Rome. While it is true that there are more than ten nations in Europe today whose territory was once part of the "Holy Roman Empire," nevertheless they may still be placed in ten groups, by reason of the languages they speak; for they represent ten principal tongues, namely, Italian, Hispanic, French, German, English, Scandinavian, Slavic, Magyar, Turkish, and Greek. Note also that in the days of the *subdivisions* of this fourth world-empire (Rome), appeared the rightful Kingdom of God—in each of these symbolic pictures—and that it is to have "everlasting dominion." Hence these two visions must picture the very same thing, namely, the full period of Gentile dominion—the "seven times" during which Zion would be in national eclipse—which is to be followed by the return of divine favor to Zion and the setting up of an "everlasting Kingdom" by divine decree; from which all peoples of earth shall be blessed.

Daniel Foresaw "The Time of the End"

In the last chapter of Daniel's prophecy he tells us that he was commanded to "shut up the words, and seal the book, even to the time of the end: many shall run to and fro, and knowledge shall be increased." (Dan. 12:4.) He also says, "And at that time shall Michael stand up, the great Prince which standeth for the children of thy people: and there shall be a time of trouble, such as never was since there was a nation: and at that time thy people shall be delivered." (vs. 1.)

Here are three things which the prophet thus described would be in evidence at "the time of the end" —the time when God's chastisement upon His people would end, and when they shall be delivered—namely: (1) "many shall run to and fro," (2) "knowledge shall be increased," and (3) "at that time . . there shall be a time of trouble, such as never was since there was a nation." If the prophet was given a truly prophetic vision of "the time of the end," and if we are now living in that time of the end, then we should be able to behold the fulfilment of these three things which he saw back there in his vision. Do we today see anything that corresponds to these matters which Daniel thus cryptically describes? Let us see.

(1) There never has been a time in all human history when humanity could "run to and fro" as at the present time, because never before did they possess such means of transportation as we enjoy today. Quick and general travel is peculiar to our time. Our grandfathers walked, or rode horseback, or used ox carts; and thus it was throughout all past history —until the last century. Then, for the first time, railway systems were built, speedy ocean liners were launched, electric cars came into use, then automobiles, bus lines, and now airplane travel. Daniel saw all this in vision, and declared that when "many shall run to and fro" it will be "the time of the end."

(2) Daniel also said that in the time of the end "knowledge shall be increased." But has not knowledge always been increasing? Not very much. Up until the last century we did not have free school systems; hence throughout all past ages the vast majority could not read or write. Nor did they have ready means of communicating knowledge even if they could have read. It is only within recent times that we have witnessed a general increase in knowledge. After the establishment of our modern free school systems came compulsory education laws, re-

quiring children to go to school and be educated. Then came the development of telegraphy, the laying of trans-oceanic cables, the establishment of great news systems, the daily newspapers, an increase in magazines and books, the establishment of free libraries, the building of telephone lines, then wireless telegraphy, the motion picture, radio communication, the talking picture, and now television. Daniel saw in vision this great day when "knowledge shall be increased" phenomenally; and said that it would be evidence of "the time of the end."

The Time of Trouble

(3) "And at that time," says Daniel, "there shall be a time of trouble, such as never was since there was a nation." It cannot be denied that the World War, which broke out so suddenly in 1914, just at the end of the "seven times" heretofore mentioned, was a conflict such as never had been known since there was a nation. It was the first and only *World* War this earth has ever seen. Daniel does not explain just what kind of trouble he saw in "the time of the end"; but if he saw no more than what humanity has witnessed since 1914, it could well be said to have been "a time of trouble such as never was since there was a nation."

But it may be that more trouble still lies ahead, and that Daniel saw it all in vision. The trouble that is to accompany this day of transition may be as "travail" (Isa. 66:6-9); that is, in successive spasms, with periods of easement in between. If so, then matters today seem to be running true to form. Came the War, a worldwide spasm; then an easement. Then came the Depression, also worldwide; and maybe another easement is ahead. Then may there not be another severe birthpang, before nations learn that might does not make right and that disregard of the rights of others does not produce lasting happiness for anybody?

Yes, it seems that we are actually in "the time of the end," exactly as the prophet saw it in vision; and that beyond the troubles attending this day of adjustment, will come peace for Zion and for the whole world. Thus declares another prophet: "In the last days it shall come to pass that . . . many nations shall come and say, Come, and let us go up to the mountain of the Lord, to the house of the God of Jacob; and He will teach us of His ways, and we will walk in His paths: for the law shall go forth out of Zion, and the word of the Lord from Jerusalem. And He shall judge among many people, and rebuke strong nations afar off; and they shall beat their swords into plowshares, and their spears into pruninghooks: nations shall not lift up sword against nation, neither shall they learn war any more."— Micah 4: 1-3.

Gentile Interest in Zionism

Fair minded Gentiles, especially in America, are becoming interested in the rights of Jewry in Palestine. The Pro-Palestine Federation of America is an organization of non-Jews pledged to aid the Jewish settlement of the holy land.

As early as 1889, before even the Jewish world had heard much of Theodor Herzl and of the Zionist movement, the late Charles Russell, a Gentile friend of Jewry and a deep student of the Hebrew prophecies, published a book in which he predicted that 1914 would mark an important change in the affairs of all Gentile nations, and particularly for God's chosen people Israel; because he believed that God's "set time" to remember Zion had come. In 1910, upon his return from Palestine where he had made friends with Dr. Levy of the Zionist organization and had addressed an interested audience of Jews in Jerusalem, some American Zionists, mainly on Dr. Levy's recommendations, allowed him to address a Jewish mass meeting at the New York Hippodrome.

More than 4,000 representative Jews attended this
unusual gathering in New York, to hear a Gentile
address them on their own Hebrew Scriptures relating to the restoration of Zion. It was a strangely
impressive event. Many, as they entered the hall,
obviously were suspicious and skeptical. No applause
greeted the speaker as he arose to address this audience; they received him in absolute silence. But
soon it became apparent that this Gentile really possessed a profound knowledge of the Hebrew Scriptures, and that he had no proselyting scheme. And
his thorough familiarity with the subject of Zionism,
and his kindly sympathy for the hopes and aspirations of Jewry soon broke down prejudice and pene-
trated the icy reserve of his hearers; and the audience that had come to debate or criticize, burst into
such a storm of applause at the finish that it literally
drowned out the music.

By a system of careful deduction based upon various Hebrew prophecies this Gentile, back in 1910,
declared to that audience of Jews his belief that
Zionism was due to take on new life shortly after the
year 1914. None at that time suspected the out-
break of a World War in that year, or at any other
time, which would wrest Palestine from the terrible
Turk and place it under the mandate of a friendly
power that would give the Jews a free hand in estab-
lishing there a Jewish Homeland. But that is exactly what occurred, much as the speaker predicted.
Among those who heard him on that occasion were
many prominent Jewish rabbis, teachers, lawyers
and editors—to mention a few by name: Dr. Jackos
and S. Goldberg, of the American Hebrew; W. J.
Solomon and J. Brodsky, of the Hebrew Standard;
Louis Lipsky, of the Maccabean; A. B. Landau, of
the Warheit; J. Pfeffer of the Jewish Weekly; Mr.
Goldman, of the Jewish Daily; S. Diamont, of the
Jewish Spirit; J. Barrondess, of the Jewish Big
Stick; Leo Wolfson, President of the Roumanian

Societies; and many others of prominence, who made it a representative audience of Jewish culture and scholarship.

This Gentile next addressed another Jewish mass meeting at the Brooklyn Academy of Music. The place was packed, with 300 crowded onto the stage, and over 2,000 had to be turned away at the doors. From there he went abroad and addressed a meeting of Jews in Royal Albert Hall, London; following which 5,000 requests for printed copies of his deductions on Zionism were received within the next two weeks. Already, it seemed, Zionism was actually beginning to take on new life; and the movement, which had been purely political in its inception, was now finding strong confirmation from a religious point of view, and enlisting many new adherents who up to this time had taken slight notice of it.

Prophecy Vitalizes the "Dry Bones"

Dr. Herzl, whose name is a household word among all friends of Zionism, had quickened national aspirations and struck a popular chord in the hearts of Jewry the world over, by stressing the political and economic advantages of a Jewish state. The ancient prophecies which had predicted the ultimate restoration of Zion had been largely overlooked or forgotten in those early days of the movement. But Dr. Herzl himself, and many other leaders, came to recognize that the religious aspect of the movement also was to be a factor of great force in the establishment of a Jewish Homeland. It is to be regretted, however, that this phase of the Zionist movement has not been given greater prominence heretofore.

Dr. Nordau, the immediate successor of Dr. Herzl, although a man of great talent and patriotic zeal, met with much difficulty in his efforts to carry on. Zionism, as a patriotic movement, was admittedly languishing. The leaders saw it trembling in the balances, and were frankly afraid that it would come to naught. It seemed that it had spent its force along the purely political lines in which it had been conceived and inaugurated. But when Jews, possessed of faith in the ancient prophets, came to see that Zionism is fulfilling the destiny of God's chosen people Israel, they with renewed zeal swung their moral force back of the movement, giving life and sinew to that which had begun to resemble a valley of dry bones. It called to mind the words of the prophet Ezekiel:

"The hand of the Lord was upon me, and carried me out in the spirit of the Lord, and set me down into the midst of the valley which was full of bones. . . . Then He said unto me, Son of man, these bones are the whole house of Israel: behold, they say, Our bones are dried, and our hope is lost. . . . Therefore *prophesy* and say unto them, Thus saith the Lord God . . . I shall put My spirit into you, and ye shall live, and I shall place you *in your own land*: then shall ye know that I the Lord have spoken it, and performed it, saith the Lord."—Ezek. 37: 1, 11, 14.

"Jacob's Trouble" Aids Zion's Rebuilding

Zionism cannot fail, for it has the backing of almighty God. He has committed Himself, through His holy prophets, to see to it that the faithful of Israel and of Judah who desire to repossess their homeland shall be permitted to do so. Although further Jewish persecutions may be anticipated in certain quarters, nevertheless "Jacob's trouble" will not dismay true Zionists; they should expect God to permit "hunters" as well as "fishers" to be instrumental in Zion's restoration. (Jer. 16: 14-17.) The prophet elsewhere says:

"For, lo, the days come, saith the Lord, that I will bring again the captivity of My people Israel and Judah, saith the Lord; and they shall possess it. . . .

Wherefore do I see every man with his hands on his loins, as a woman in travail, and all faces are turned into paleness? Alas! for that day is great, so that none is like it: it is even the time of *Jacob's trouble*; but he shall be saved out of it. . . .

"Therefore fear thou not, O My servant Jacob, saith the Lord; neither be dismayed, O Israel; for, lo, I will save thee from afar, and thy seed from the land of their captivity; and Jacob shall return, and shall be in rest, and be quiet, and none shall make him afraid. For I am with thee, saith the Lord, to save thee: though I make a full end of all nations whither I have scattered thee, yet I will not make a full end of thee: but I will correct thee in measure, and will not leave thee altogether unpunished. . . . Why criest thou for thine affliction? . . . For I will restore health unto thee, and I will heal thee of thy wounds, saith the Lord; because they called thee an outcast, saying, This is Zion, whom no man seeketh after . . . in the *latter days* ye shall consider it."— Jer. 30: 3-24.

Evidently the "hunters" of Germany, Poland, Roumania and elsewhere have not yet succeeded in driving to Palestine all the Jews whom the Lord would have return there for the rehabilitation of the homeland. It is equally evident that many of Jewry in friendly lands must yet be aroused by the "fishers" who are being sent to attract them into the Zionist fold. It is confidently expected that many other Jews of wealth or of a pioneering spirit—especially those having an abiding faith in the foregoing promises— will either join with the Mizrachi World Organization or otherwise assist in forwarding the work of Zionism as soon as they come to realize that this movement is of God and is clearly foretold through the ancient prophets of Israel. In this day of turmoil, coincident with the termination of the Gentile lease of power and the great "time of trouble" heretofore mentioned, **great financial upheavals may be** expected; and those of Israel who have the means, but who hold back from supporting this movement which is ordained of God, may find themselves in the condition of those mentioned by the prophet Ezekiel: "They shall cast their silver in the streets, and their gold shall be removed; their silver and their gold shall not be able to deliver them in the day of the wrath of the Lord."—Ezek. 7:19.

Who Has the Faith of Abraham?

The great "Messenger of the Covenant whom ye delight in" shall test and prove all Israel as a people chosen of God. (Malachi 3:1, 3.) Those who worship idols of gold, silver, stocks, bonds or other material things, and forget their privileges and duties as the chosen of the Lord, will not only miss the opportunity of sharing in the present rebuilding of Zion in fulfilment of prophecy, but will receive severe chastisement at His hands in this day of transition—that they may be taught some much needed lessons ere He can use them as channels of blessing in fulfilment of the ancient promise to Abraham: "In thy seed shall all the nations of the earth be blessed; because thou hast obeyed My voice."—Gen. 22:18.

Those of Israel who are unwilling to obey God's voice at this time in helping to rebuild Zion, do not have the faith of Abraham; they do not possess Jacob's appreciation of God's promises; but, like Esau, they prefer the things of momentary comfort and pleasure rather than claim their divinely intended birthright. But chastisements from God are blessings in disguise; and harsh experiences during the days of "Jacob's trouble" may open the eyes and ears of many to appreciate and heed the voice of Israel's prophets. If that be so, then these providences of God can accomplish far more in rebuilding Zion than can mere economic advantages in the homeland, or purely Jewish pride or popular patriotism.

After Zion is rebuilded, then, according to the prophets, Israel's future work of extending blessings to all humanity is due to begin. God will then make a new covenant with His chosen people, even as Jeremiah has foretold: "Behold, the days come, saith the Lord, that I will make a new covenant with the house of Israel and with the house of Judah; not according to the covenant that I made with their fathers [whose mediator Moses could not give them lasting blessings] in the day I took them by the hand and led them out of Egypt, which covenant they brake . . . but I will put My law in their inward parts, and write it in their hearts; and will be their God, and they shall be My people."—Jer. 31:31-33.

Moses declared that a greater than he would ultimately lead the people. (Deut. 18:15.) Moses, of course, referred to the coming Messiah of Israel. Similarly David declared, "The Lord shall send the rod of thy strength out of Zion. . . . The Lord hath sworn and will not repent, Thou art a priest forever, after the order of Melchizedek . . . He shall judge among the Gentiles . . . He shall wound the heads over many countries." (Psalms 110.) May it not be that this great Messiah, "the King of glory," is a heavenly Lord, who even now is overruling the work of rebuilding Zion, preparatory to re-establishing the throne of David, and ultimately exercising spiritual dominion worldwide?

Israel's Double

In an earlier part of this treatise we discussed the prophecies relating to the "seven times" of national chastisement upon Jewry, and offered the suggestion that we have now reached the end of that long period, and that this accounts for the origin and present impetus of the Zionist movement. Another prophecy of interest to God's chosen people is the hitherto obscure utterance of Zechariah, who wrote these words a few years after the Babylonian captivity: "Shout, O daughter of Jerusalem: behold, thy King cometh unto thee; he is just and having salvation; lowly and riding upon an ass . . . turn ye to the strong hold, ye prisoners of hope: even today do I declare, I will render *double* unto thee."—Zech. 9: 9-12.

Another equally strange prophecy which evidently refers to the same matter, is the following passage from Isaiah: "Speak ye comfortably to Jerusalem, and cry unto her, that her warfare is accomplished, that her iniquity is pardoned: for she hath received of the Lord's hand *double* for all her sins." (Isaiah 40: 2.) Although the word *mishneh* was used in the Zechariah prophecy, and *kephel* is the word employed by Isaiah, yet the meaning undoubtedly is the same—each text referring to a period or to an experience, or both, which would be a *duplication* or repetition of something that had gone before. Zechariah foretells this "double" before it happens, while Isaiah prophesied of the time when the "double" would be ended and when Zion would again come into her own.

Zechariah does not say, in his prophecy, when the "double" is to begin; he merely quotes the Lord as saying, "even today do I declare, I *will* [future from the prophet's day] render *double unto thee*"— he does not say, "Today the double begins." Nor does Isaiah say when this "double" would end—he merely declares that when it does end Jerusalem shall be "comforted," because the "set time" would then have arrived when God shall return His kind favor to Zion. What then does this "double" refer to, and when does it begin and terminate? Inasmuch as Isaiah shows that divine favor was to be withheld from Jerusalem during this "double," therefore this period of punishment must coincide, at least in part, with the full period of the "seven times" of disfavor heretofore mentioned. But this "double" of disfavor could not have begun at the same date that the "seven times" began; that is, at the time when the Jewish kingdom ended, at the Babylonian captivity. Why?

Because Zechariah was a *post-exile* prophet, writing several years after the Babylonian captivity had ended; and he says that this "double" had not yet begun, that it would be declared upon Jewry at some date in the future. If the "double" had begun at the time of the captivity and the destruction of Jerusalem, then undoubtedly the prophecy would have said, "I have rendered," instead of, "I *will* render double unto thee."

The Dispersion

Evidently, therefore, this "double" of disfavor has reference to some additional national punishment that was to come upon the Jews as a people at some time subsequent to the Babylonian captivity. But what could it signify? What chastisement ever came upon Jewry that was greater than that suffered in 606 B. C., when her children were taken captive to Babylon, her kingdom overthrown, and her temple and capital city destroyed? We answer: The Dispersion, of A. D. 70-73, was far more terrible than the captivity of 606 B. C. After that Babylonian captivity the Jews were permitted to return to Palestine; and while they were not allowed to restore the kingdom, yet they did maintain a tributary national existence in their own land for the next six hundred years—until they were ruthlessly dispersed into all the world by the Roman legions under Titus. This dispersion began in 70 A. D., but the last Jewish fortification did not surrender until the morning of the Passover, 73 A. D.

Was this, then, the ultimate practical beginning of the "double" of disfavor? It would seem so. While divine disfavor clearly began prior to this time, yet this was the date when its actual and terrible manifestation became pronounced. Like certain other epochs in Biblical history, this "double" may be regarded as having two or three beginnings and two or three endings, like overlapping cycles. But it seems clear that the ultimate beginning of this "double" of disfavor was when the Jewish fort of Masada surrendered in 73 A. D., and the Jews were absolutely uprooted from their land of promise and finally dispersed to other lands afar. Since that date the Jews have never had even a semblance of national existence as a people—until the beginning of the present rehabilitation of the Jewish Homeland under the Zionists, within the last few years.

National Existence—National Eclipse

But why is this period of complete national annihilation of Jewry, from the time of the Dispersion until now, called a "double"? A double, or duplication, of what? Since this is seen to have been a period of total absence of national existence for Jewry, it would then seem that it is called a "double" simply because it is a duplication, in point of time, of the period during which Israel enjoyed a national existence. And how long did she exist as a nation? Her early beginning dates from the death of Jacob, at which time "the twelve tribes of Israel" came to be recognized as such, and dwelt together as "the house of Israel."

Historians compute the death of Jacob as being about two centuries before the Exodus from Egypt. The long period of time from then down to A. D. 73 has been so definitely recorded in the Scriptures and in secular history that scholars agree to its exact length to within less than 20 years—some holding that 1813 B. C. was the correct date of Jacob's death, while others compute it as being 1794 B. C. But whichever date we take, the "double" of that period is found to touch down here at the time in which we are now living, and when the Zionist movement is being so outstandingly blessed by the Lord.

Taking into consideration the suggestion already made, that there is probably an overlapping of cycles in connection with this "double" of time—since it may be regarded as having a preliminary beginning when the circumstances first arose which ultimately led up to the complete Dispersion of Israel in 70-73 A. D.—it brings the "beginning of the end" of the double at about the time when the Zionist movement originated and began to grow to its present important proportions.

We do not need to insist upon the absolute accuracy of any past dates, nor do we attempt here to make predictions for any future ones. It is sufficient for our purpose if these calculations are only approximately correct. That being so, they do furnish a reasonable basis for belief that here again is prophetic corroboration of the fact that "the time to favor Zion, yea, the *set* time, is come" (Psalm 102: 13), and that the time for the fulfilment of Isaiah's prophecy is at hand:

"O Zion, Lift Up Thy Voice!"

"Comfort ye, comfort ye, My people, saith your God. Speak ye comfortably to Jerusalem, and cry unto her that her warfare is accomplished, that her iniquity is pardoned: for she hath received of the Lord's hand DOUBLE for all her sins. . . . O Zion, that bringest good tidings, get thee up into the high mountain; O Jerusalem, that bringest good tidings, lift up thy voice with strength; lift it up; be not afraid; say unto the cities of Judah, Behold your God! . . . Behold, the nations are as a drop of a bucket, and are counted as the small dust of the balance: behold, He taketh up the isles as a very little thing. . . . All nations before Him are as nothing; and they are counted to Him less than nothing, and vanity. . . . Why sayest thou, O Jacob, and speakest, O Israel, My way is hid from the Lord, and my judgment is passed over from my God? . . . He giveth power to the faint; and to them that have no might He increaseth strength."—Isa. 40: 1, 2, 9, 15, 17, 27-29.

Transforming a Waste into a Garden

During the period of the present generation we have witnessed the gradual rise of Zionism—from a visionary theory in the mind of Theodor Herzl and his co-workers, to the practical establishment of a Jewish National Home through the cooperation of Jews the world over. About in the middle of this period of rise, came the wresting of Palestine from the Turk, the Balfour Declaration and the British mandate, since which time the actual rebuilding of the Homeland has begun in dead earnest. The greatest progress has been made during the past ten years. But there is much yet to be done; and the funds raised during the present drive will make possible the carrying forward of pending plans for the receiving of additional hundreds of thousands of Jews into this Homeland within the next few years.

The World War of 1914-18 had left Palestine economically in very desperate straits. The Turkish armies had plundered and devastated the towns and rural districts as well. But this was nothing new; for throughout long centuries of political and religious strife her agricultural resources had been ravished by contending Turks and Arabs, and her forests also ruthlessly destroyed. Little or no effort ever had been made to maintain soil productivity or prevent soil erosion; and nothing had been done towards irrigation, outside the crude hand-made efforts of a few individual Arabs. Impoverished and depopulated by almost two millennia of misrule and inadequate cultivation, the holy land's original natural endowments had become nearly nonexistent.

The World War completed the wreck, so that 1918 found Palestine almost destitute of plant and animal life, with 50 per cent of her land written off as barren. The census taken in 1920 revealed only 80,000 head of cattle, 4,000 mules, and a few camels in the whole country. It was a common sight there to see a man or a woman, instead of an animal, hitched to a plough. In 1922 the Director of Agriculture of Palestine reported the total of exploitable land surface to be not exceeding 7,000 square miles.

Then the "hunters" of Jeremiah 16:16 appeared, and drove numerous Jews from Russia, Poland, Roumania and Germany, back to their homeland. These Jewish refugees started reclaiming the arid land, so that by 1930 the Commissioner of Lands gave in his report for Palestine 612,000 acres of farm land; 375,000 hill acres; and in the Beersheba area 1,025,500 acres. Obviously no figure can be accepted yet as final for the total of "cultivable" land there until the Jewish farmer has defined the word "cultivable." These figures did not include the swamps nor coastal marshes, the sand dunes, nor the rocky hills between Rafa and Acre, nor the Wilderness of Judea; these were considered as a cipher.

Since then what has this ancient people of the "shop" done about farming in Palestine? Well! within a few short years the Jew has drained and brought to a high state of cultivation 211,800 acres of swamps of Samaria. These malaria-infested miles of "no man's land," whose pools were the breeding beds of death-dealing insects and disease, have become a garden, irrigated and planted in fruits. A land previously without an inhabitant and called "cursed" by many people, is now laden with the perfume of the orange and lemon tree. These cesspools of the coasts have changed into an Eden of citrus-bearing trees whose blossoms make a panorama of delight, and whose fruits have brought new hope to a long exiled and seemingly forgotten people.

Divine Providence Over Jewry

But the Jew should not forget that the battle has not been his; that while he fought, the God of his fathers also fought beside him, and has begun to fulfil His ancient promise and "hath given the increase."

The antitypical year of Jubilee has come, the "trumpet" is now sounding, calling every Jew to return to his possession; and all the captives are to be set free.

"Lo, the day has come, saith the Lord, the day when I said I will bring again the captivity of My people Israel and Judah; I will cause them to return to the land that I gave to their fathers and they shall possess it. . . . Ye shall buy fields in this land, whereof ye say, It is desolate, without man or beast, it is given into the hands of the Chaldeans; men shall buy fields for money, and subscribe evidences and seal them, and take witnesses, in the land of Benjamin, and in the places about Jerusalem, in the cities of Judah, in the cities of the mountains: for I will cause thy captivity to return, saith the Lord." "Thou shalt build the waste cities and inhabit them; thou shalt plant vineyards and drink the wine thereof; thou shalt make gardens and eat the fruit of them.

"I will plant you upon the land and thou shalt no more be pulled out of the land which I have given thee." "I will call for the corn and I will increase it, and lay no famine upon you. I will multiply the fruit of thy trees and the increase of thy fields." "I will open rivers in high places, and fountains in the midst of the valleys. I will make the wilderness a pool of water, and the dry land springs of water." "Thou shalt build houses and inhabit them: thou shalt plant vineyards and eat the fruit of them: thou shalt not build and another inhabit, thou shalt not plant and another eat; thou shalt not labor in vain nor bring forth for trouble . . . for thou art the seed of the Blessed of the Lord."

"In the day that I have cleansed you from all your iniquities, I will cause you to dwell in the cities, and the wastes shall be builded, the desolate land shall be tilled whereas it lay desolate in the sight of all that passed by; and they shall say, This land that was desolate is become like the Garden of Eden, and the waste and desolate and ruined cities are become fenced and are inhabited." "And thou shalt dwell in the land that I gave unto Jacob my servant, wherein your fathers have dwelt; and ye shall dwell therein, even thou and thy children and their children's children forever.

"My servant David shall be thy Prince and I will be thy God forever." "Ye shall go out with joy and be led forth with peace: the mountains and hills shall break forth before you into singing, and all the trees of the field shall clap their hands. Instead of the thorn shall come up the fir tree, instead of the brier the myrtle: and it shall be to the Lord for a name, for an everlasting sign that shall not be cut off." "In the wilderness I will plant the cedar, the shittam tree, the myrtle and the olive. In the desert I will plant the fir and the pine and the box tree. All shall see, and know and consider and understand together that the hand of the Lord hath done this; the Holy One of Israel hath created it."—Jer. 30:32; Amos 9; Ezek. 36:35; Isa. 41:18.

Israel, go up, possess ye your land. Be of good courage, and believe in Him who hath promised, for He is able and ready to fulfil all these things.

Zionist Progress

While millions have been invested by the various Jewish organizations, created for the very purpose of making a national home of the land of their fathers, a place of refuge for the hunted and persecuted of Jewry; yet it is no part of the Zionist scheme to encourage pauperism or indiscriminate charity. The ideal is to create a self-respecting co-operative commonwealth in which every one shall pull his share of the weight, producing his own food, clothing, tools to carry on, and the necessities of life. One of the fundamental planks in the undertaking is that all land bought from the Gentiles is to remain forever in the hands of the Jews. It cannot be resold to an alien. Furthermore a lease or homestead can be for only

49 years; then in the 50th year it returns to the original Jewish Land Co. But the lessee can renew his lease if he so wishes. The amount of land each Jew may obtain under this arrangement is determined by how much he can work individually without hiring help. Here then are three death knells for the old order—to speculation, to exploitation, and, last but not least, to pauperism—for should old age or sickness overtake any individual, a fund created from the "lease tax" provides the hire for having his crops cultivated, harvested and marketed for him. Hence the fear of becoming homeless or dependent upon charity never disturbs his peace of mind. Those sinister twin brothers, the almshouse and the poor-farm, never come nigh his dwelling.

Zionism is thus proving to a doubting world that Jewry not only possesses the political qualities essential to self-government, but that it knows how to make every man secure and of equal size. The Jewish bodies in Palestine have spent $700,000,000 on drainage, irrigation, amelioration of soil, and afforestation. The Palestine Jewish Colonization Association is concerned with the colonization of Samaria, upper and lower Galilee and Judea. They already have reclaimed much land and established plantations throughout Judea; built highways and railroads; also water supply and irrigation systems. They have invested $30,000,000 in colonization, and $2,000,000 in the aromatic or perfume industry which is only in its infancy.

Harnessing the Jordan

The Zionist scheme of electrification of Palestine, costing millions, has now become a fact; from this all of Palestine is to have power for her various commercial interests, as well as light, heat, and irrigation. Such names as Lord Reading, Rothschild, Hirst and Mond, on the directorate of the Palestine Electric Corporation, to carry out the great Ruten-

from different parts of the country, also to the study of fertilizers, trees, seeds, livestock, poultry, insects, etc. The Agriculture Extension Department conducts lectures all over the Homeland to give everyone the benefit of discoveries made. A children's village, established in 1927, has 175 acres where these youngsters are taught truck gardening, horticulture, fruit-raising, etc., in connection with other educational studies. Here children are accepted, from kintergarten age up to the 8th grade. There is a budget of $40,000 for its annual upkeep.

The Jewish Fund has planted 1,225,000 euculyptus trees in arid areas for the stabilization of the sands. Such trees are used along the railway between Egypt and Palestine for protective purposes. Between 1920-29 over 5,000,000 trees and 2,000,000 vines were planted throughout the Homeland, most of which were from Government nurseries.

Thousands of New Enterprises

Already there are over 3,500 different enterprises now existing in Palestine, more than 2,000 of which were never heard of there up to a few years ago. The Palestine Potash Co. Ltd., is extracting minerals from the Dead Sea, and have found it a veritable gold mine of natural resources. It is estimated that the mineral deposits in the Dead Sea are worth at least 238 billion pounds sterling, or about 1,200 billion dollars—greater than the combined wealth of all the nations of the world.

At Haifa is located not only the newly deepened harbor, but railway workshops, sugar refineries, a match factory, a cement plant, an oil factory, and flour mills. At Jaffa is located the fine new harbor and an electric power station—part of the huge electrification scheme for which the waters of the Jordan are being used—also soap factories, etc. Great brick works are at Tel-Aviv. Bethlehem is the home of the textile industry, furniture factories, etc. At Nazareth, farther to the north, are engineering shops, printing plants, an ice factory and mineral works. Near Jerusalem is the home of the red marble industry. Altogether there are now 265 flour mills, and hundreds of other important enterprises too numerous to mention. There are over 600 olive oil mills which manufacture numerous products; also textile mills, tobacco and gypsum industries, tanneries, etc. Private investments in all these undertakings, exclusive of colonization itself, amounts to $51,000,000.

The importance of all this lies in the fact that these pioneers are the forerunners of an established Zionist commonwealth. As such, they should be appraised; not by old world standards but by pioneering standards; for they are but the vanguard of later and greater achievements. However, even now their work in the field of agriculture is exciting the attention of other peoples in various parts of the world.

Palestine's institutions for research, her laboratories, experimental farms, unique credit system, scientific agricultural literature, etc., also her fine harbors and her highways and rapid transportation lines—already established or in the process of construction—all point the way to future Jewish colonization on a large scale. So expert are the methods employed in the Homeland that a fair-sized Jewish family can exist in comparative comfort on as little as two and one-half acres of ground. The words "depression" and "unemployment" are quite unknown among these pioneers.

The Unquenchable Fire of Faith

But this story of the rebuilding of the Jewish Homeland would be far from complete if merely these commercial achievements were recorded. Zion would be "as sounding brass and tinkling cymbals" were it not for those vital elements of *faith* in the ancient promises of restoration, which well up within the heart of the faithful of Israel, and for which prayers have ascended for centuries while rivers of tears have flowed. Soon after the first mad rush for a foothold in Palestine had been accomplished—which at first was but as a peg on which to hang one's hat—the hitherto latent spiritual side of Zionism also began to manifest itself.

An eye witness tells of the pent-up longings of ages that broke all bounds at the laying of the cornerstone of the Hebrew University there a few years ago. Whether Zionist or non-Zionist, Jew or Gentile, it was impossible not to recognize the real source and depth of that heart-cry as those pioneers of the Homeland, and their kinsmen from afar, began to realize this further beginning of their hitherto oft-deferred hope of emancipation. "Never," said this witness, "have I ever seen a crowd so reveal its inner self. Men stood transfixed, women wept; and no one slept nor talked anything else for days, but this momentous event, this cornerstone, of Zion!" It was on Mt. Scopus—the Mount of Olives—overlooking the ancient capital, Jerusalem, that Dr. Chaim Weizmann, head of the World Zionist Organization, in the presence of Lord Balfour, General Allenby, Albert Einstein, and representative Jews from all parts of the world, laid the foundation of this all-Jewish institution of learning, as a symbol that God, through Israel, shall soon give light unto all the earth. Not one stone, but twelve, were laid; symbolizing the cooperation of the twelve tribes as one people.

An Advanced Centre of Learning

In 1927 Prof. Albert Einstein accepted the chair of Professor of Sciences in this Hebrew University. He has since endowed a chair for the study of the higher sciences, to extend beyond the field covered by the curriculum of other universities; which makes this new Hebrew University at Jerusalem the most advanced seat of learning in the world today. Nor does this University limit itself to Jewish students;

it opens its doors to all people, regardless of race, creed or color; thus offering exceptional educational facilities to all, untrammeled by sectarian policies.

No sooner had the University begun to function when substantial contributions of equipment began to arrive, to help make it the truly great institution it is destined to become. Prof. Ignaz Goltziher released to it the famous Oriental Library, with its 6,000 volumes. Then the equally famous Chezanvitch Library, of Bielostock, containing 5,000 volumes in 16 languages, was transferred to the University. The French Government sent a contribution of very valuable books. The Fecheimer family, of Cincinnati, donated 6,000 volumes, Oscar Straus gave 500 volumes, and various others. Also the Dutch Government has instructed various universities in the Netherlands to make certain valuable donations of books, some extremely rare volumes; and already nearly 1,000 copies have been received from this source, with promise of others to come. It is the expectation that this rapidly growing library of the University of Jerusalem will become the greatest and finest scholastic library in the world. And the Jewish pioneers of the Homeland are quick to take advantage of their educational opportunities. Not only is the University library well patronized, but it is not uncommon to see a Jewish lad plowing his field and at the same time carrying in his pocket, for instant perusal during moments of leisure, a Hebrew translation of Homer's *Iliad* or some other classic.

The Regathering of All Israel

Palestine, within its present confined limits, of course would not be capable of receiving but a portion of the 17,000,000 Jews now living upon the earth. Nor is it expected that all Jews will endeavor to return to the Homeland. Many, indeed, have lost faith in the divine promises made to God's people through the prophets of old, or otherwise are not yet fully sympathetic with the endeavors and objectives of Zionism. But this is no argument against the success of the movement. Nor is the fact that certain Jews are firmly established in other lands, and have no immediate desire to reside in Palestine, any reason why they should not at least be deeply interested in the establishment of a Homeland for those Jews who do wish to return thither. It should bring joy to the heart of every man and woman, in whose veins flow the lifeblood of Abraham and of Jacob, to know that somewhere on this earth is a land that Jews may call their own. And should not that joy be intensified many fold by knowledge of the fact that such a homeland is now actually in process of rehabilitation, and that it is none other than the very land made sacred by Israel's ancient patriarchs and prophets, where ruled the judges who sat in Moses' seat, and where reigned the kings of the illustrious Davidic line?

Before Messiah's Kingdom can be established, at least a remnant of the faithful of all Israel must be regathered to Palestine, even as the prophets have declared. Isaiah identifies Israel's Messiah as a righteous One unto whom "shall the Gentiles seek." (Isa. 11:10.) Then he continues: "And it shall come to pass in that day, that the Lord shall set His hand again, the second time [even as He did the first time, at the end of the Babylonian captivity], to recover the remnant of His people. . . . And He shall set up an ensign for the nations, and shall assemble the outcasts of Israel, and gather together the dispersed of Judah, *from the four corners of the earth.*"—Isa. 11:11, 12.

Already hundreds of thousands of the dispersed of Jewry have been regathered to the Homeland. The Jewish *halutzim* or pioneers, who now are in Palestine, have come from no less than 64 different nations; although the majority are from eastern and central Europe, where orthodox Judaism flourishes more than in the West. And yet it is largely through the contributions of the more prosperous Jews of the West that the rapid rebuilding of this ancient Homeland is being made possible. Immigration is progressing as fast as funds will allow—over 61,000 Jews having entered Palestine during the past twelve months. This immigration began on an important scale in 1925. In that year, for the first time in twenty-five centuries since the "seven times" of Jewry's affliction began, the flag of Judah and the star of David floated over the seas—atop the mast of the S. S. President Arthur, on her maiden voyage as one of the American-Palestine lines.

A Remnant of All Tribes

These Jews who now are returning to Palestine undoubtedly are remnants of all twelve tribes. Even the tribe of Dan, which separated from their brethren and migrated into Arabia after the captivity, where they have roamed as nomads for the past twenty-four hundred years, now have folded their tents and returned to their ancient homeland and have settled in a colony near Jerusalem, happy and full of faith in the belief that Zionism—the "Third Jewish Commonwealth"—heralds the near approach of Messiah's Kingdom.

A large part of the regathered of Israel who are now in Palestine are truly called *halutzim*—pioneers, or the advance guard. These men and women, animated by faith, hope and patriotism, are gladly enduring all needful privations for the cause of Zion. All through the country you will see them, in companies large and small, working with an idealism that has never been seen before. You will see educators, college professors, lawyers, and doctors of philosophy, doing their share alongside more hardy laborers, all engaged in breaking stone, mixing cement, and laying highways. And after a hard day's work of this sort they will assemble and sing the triumphal songs of Zion. Such sacrificial service is not for mercenary reasons; it is due to a spiritual urge, and it animates the hearts of thousands.

Like the Zeal of the Ancients

With many of these, their sacrifices began long before they reached Palestine. Many poor Jews from Russia, Poland, Roumania, Germany and elsewhere, had to undergo intense suffering and endure the greatest of privations, before they finally succeeded in accomplishing their supreme desire—that of coming here to assist in rehabilitating this Jewish Homeland. An able engineer from Russia arrived without shoes, his feet bandaged in old rags. It had taken him eleven long months through cold and heat to make the journey on foot. But he got there, and was joyful that he could come and have a part with the other happy *halutzim* in rebuilding Zion.

When Dr. Herzl, over forty years ago, envisioned Palestine as a free homeland for the persecuted of Jewry, few realized or even dared hope that it would really become an accomplished fact within this generation. They mourned for Zion, and waited; they did not then know that God's "set time to favor her" really had come. (Psa. 102:13.) They did not suspect the meaning of the "seven times" of chastisement, nor that this period of Gentile domination had about run its course. (Lev. 26: 18, 24, 28.) They did not realize that Israel's "warfare is accomplished, that her iniquity is pardoned: for she hath received of the Lord's hand *double* for all her sins." (Isa. 40:2.) Nevertheless Dr. Herzl and his associates began—no one knew exactly why—to frantically appeal to Jewish pride, to instill patriotism into God's chosen people the world over, to establish Zionist societies in all countries, and to educate and enthuse all Jewry for possible great developments ahead.

The Zionist idea seemed too fantastic at first. How could a handful of persecuted Jews ever hope to **gain a foothold in this despoiled** land which the terrible Turk holds in a deathlike grip? And how could Jews expect to make a living there if they did find entrance? But those who thus doubted the practicability of Zionist hopes in those days were reckoning without a knowledge of God's plan for His chosen people. Others simply held on somehow by blind faith. And finally the "set time" arrived for God to perform His "strange act." Came 1914, the end of the "seven times," the World War, the capture of Jerusalem, the wresting of all Palestine from beneath the ruthless heel of the Turk, and the opening of this ancient fatherland to immigration and to the establishment of a Jewish National Home. It was the beginning of Jewry's emancipation, and the "beginning of the end" of Gentile domination over Zion.

A Deliverance Not Merely of Man

When Jerusalem was captured from the Turks in 1917, not merely Jewry but the whole wide world thrilled to the news of the event. Everybody seemed to sense that here was some unusual history in the making—as if some strange spiritual current had sent a wave of wonder around the entire earth. Even the British troops themselves were peculiarly affected as on no other battlefield, said Sir Arthur Wingate; all being eager for information as to the history of each town or hill as it was taken. And so keenly interested was the reading public the world over, concerning this sector of the allied campaign, that the army of newspaper correspondents were kept busy for days thumbing through Bibles, fitting Old Testament records to current events, and cabling column after column of dispatches filled with narrations of things that occurred on this same battlefield far back in the great days of the Jewish kingdom.

If the capture of Jerusalem thus excited the attention of all Gentile peoples throughout the earth, how indeed must it have thrilled every Jew—especially he who is filled with a traditional passion for the land of his fathers, so great that he instinctively turns his face toward Jerusalem when he prays; who buries his dead facing east; and who purposely leaves partly unfinished every house that he builds for his dwelling, as mute testimony to the fact that he is but a sojourner, a wanderer, a pilgrim in a strange land not his own! Even Lord Rothschild, one of the world's wealthiest bankers, left unfinished one of the pillars in his palatial home, thus signifying his role as a child of the dispersion, with but a temporary abiding place, and symbolizing his hope that some day Israel may be able to fold her tents and go back home.

How Jerusalem Was Spared

How Jerusalem was taken on December 9, 1917, without bombs or gunfire, seems nothing short of a divine miracle. Jerusalem is almost impregnable as a natural fortress or stronghold. The Turkish army could have held out for quite a long time, inflicting many casualties upon the allies. In the end, the city might have been destroyed, even as it was laid low by Nebuchadnezzar at the beginning of the "seven times," and by Titus at the beginning of the "double." But the time had come for God to deal "comfortably" with Jerusalem; for "her warfare is accomplished, her iniquity is pardoned; for she hath received of the Lord's hand *double* for all her sins." (Isa. 40:1, 2.) Hence, in divine providence, not only was the city spared from destruction but it was actually taken without a single shot being fired; though it was being held by fierce and modernly equipped Turkish troops.

It was not until after the armistice that the full story behind Jerusalem's easy capture came to light. As General Allenby approached with his army, he wondered how he could best take the city without too much damage. He had no desire to destroy it, and in fact abhorred the thought of devastation and bloodshed within its sacred walls. But war is war, and

he had a duty to perform. While thus he was trying
to formulate plans for capturing yet sparing the city,
an enemy runner reached his Turkish commandant,
and reported that a strong army was approaching,
led by a powerful general named Allah-Bey (Allenby). The news quickly spread among the super-
stitious Moslem troops, and the magic name Allenby
was understood by all of them to be *Allah-Bey*—
which meant, "The prophet of Allah." Terrified by
what to them was a sacred name, they refused to
fight against a "prophet of Allah," fearing Allah's
displeasure; and the commandant finally gave orders
to hastily evacuate the holy city ere "Allah-Bey"
arrived.

The Clock of the Ages Strikes

General Allenby, on taking over the occupation of
the city permitted the residents to resume their peaceful pursuits with little interruption. But one important change was that of abolishing the Mohamme-
dan Hegira calendar, which had held sway over this
land for 1335 years, and putting into effect the Gre-
gorian calendar, beginning January 1, 1918. Mean-
while General Allenby, and the "Jewish Legion"
fighting under the Jewish flag, pressed on, clearing
the Turks from the remainder of Palestine. Evidently
General Allenby's name had lost its magic, as the
Turks came to understand it better; and the legion
now met with considerable resistance. But they held
all the territory, from Gaza in the south to Beersheba in the north. By autumn Damascus was occupied. And just as the Jewish Legion succeeded in
driving the Turks beyond the ancient Solomon-Da-
vidic boundary near Damascus, thus emancipating
the entire land from this people who for centuries
has been the chief thorn in Israel's side, the general
armistice was declared. It was as if God had said,
"The main objective, so far as My chosen people
are concerned, is now accomplished; hence cease

your hostilities, and let them go up and rebuild their homeland."

After Jerusalem was destroyed in A. D. 70, Hebrew ceased to be the spoken language of the land. Now that the "double" has ended, this ancient tongue is being restored. For several years Prof. Eliezer Ben Yewdah, an ardent Zionist who died in 1922, strove to bring it back into its own. His efforts met with little success at the first, and he was looked upon as a visionary; but he lived to see his works bearing fruit. Hebrew is now being freely spoken in the Homeland, and the schools there employ it as the medium of instruction. Postage stamps now bear the Hebrew words, *Arez Israel*—the land of Israel. The currency of Palestine no longer carries the superscription of Cæsar, or the face of a Caliph, but instead "The Tower of David." The $1,500,000 palace which the German Kaiser built on the Mount of Olives, is now a government house for the New Palestine.

Climatic Conditions Improving

Even the climatic conditions of Palestine are now showing marked improvement. In 1927 the Pools of Solomon, dry for centuries, began to overflow. At that time the High Commissioner of Palestine was asked to declare a day of public thanksgiving to God for this seeming miracle. The pools were measured and found to contain approximately sixty million gallons. In Bible times there were two copious rainy seasons in Palestine, the "early and the latter rain." But for the past many centuries the "early rains" have been scant; while the "latter rains" and the dews had disappeared completely. But now these have returned to gladden the land, with the result that some parts of Palestine now yield two or three crops a year.

The prophecy of Zechariah, written after the return from the Babylonian captivity, seems more applicable today than at any time in the past: "Thus saith the Lord, I am returned unto Zion, and will dwell in the midst of Jerusalem: and Jerusalem shall be called a city of truth. . . . Now I will be unto the residue of this people as in the former days, saith the Lord of hosts. For the seed shall be prosperous; the vine shall give her fruit, and the ground shall give her increase, and the heavens shall give her dew; and I will cause the remnant of this people to possess all these things." (Zech. 8:3, 11, 12.) "Be glad then, ye children of Zion, and rejoice in the Lord your God: for He hath given you the former rain moderately, and He will cause to come down for you the rain; the former rain, and [also] the latter rain in the first month."—Joel 2:25.

For some reason the climatic conditions of Palestine seem peculiarly suited to the Jew; he prospers where other peoples have failed. On this point we quote from an address by an able Zionist, the late Nahum Sokolow, as follows:

"To the ancient Jew, Palestine is *home*. To the Europeans going there it is a foreign land. The stalwart Prussians took their wives and tried to colonize Palestine with Prussians. The result was: Their children born in that land were puny, physically frail, sickly and weak. But the Jew who settles there, though he himself may not be robust because of years of privation and hardship elsewhere, is able to produce robust offspring in this homeland. It seems to be God's answer to those who challenge the right of the Jew to this land, which was given by God to Abraham and his seed."

Intellectual Wealth for Zion

It is recalled that a few months after the World War began, the British found themselves running short of a certain mineral product essential to high explosives; and the situation was becoming alarming. In that critical hour a Jewish chemist, who had lived in England for 25 years and taught chemistry at Cambridge, set to work in his laboratory to develop a chemical substitute—and he succeeded. The British engineers tested out this substitute and were elated, and in their extremity the government was ready to pay a fabulous price to this chemist for his valuable formula. That chemist was Dr. Chaim Weizmann, an enthusiastic Zionist, who later, and for 13 years, headed the World Zionist Organization and subsequently became President of the Hebrew University at Jerusalem. Dr. Weizmann's reply to the British government was, "I do not desire that the government pay me anything for my formula; but I do request the government to promise that they will try to free the land of Palestine from the Turk, and then secure it as a homeland for my people." The promise was given, the Turk was driven out; and the historic Balfour Declaration, the British Mandate over Palestine, and all subsequent British assistance in the establishment of the Jewish National Home, are the result.

The remnant of Jewry now returning to Palestine are bringing to the homeland great wealth, not only of substance but especially of intellect. It is no secret that Jews generally are an intelligent, progressive people. They have become leaders in practically every field they have entered. They are the world's leading bankers. They excel in commerce. They also become leading lawyers, leading scientists, leading philosophers. Some of the world's greatest musicians and composers are Jews. The same is true in the literary field; many become great authors, editors, historians, poets. The European press is largely controlled by Jewish brains, and they also are an important element in the American press.

Although Jews constitute but three percent of the population of Germany, yet no less than 100 chairs in German universities were occupied by Jews up to 1933. The world has heard much about the achievements of "German scientists"; but what is not always noted is the fact that many of these achievements are the work of Jewish minds. For example, it was Hertz, the German Jew, who proved the existence of electro-magnetic waves, that led the way to numerous electrical inventions and to the development of wireless telegraphy and radio. In America the outstanding electrical wizard was Steinmetz, an immigrant Jew from Russia.

Prosperity and "Fame in Every Land"

These achievements of Jews are mentioned, not to boast but to show the fulfilment of prophecy. Zephaniah, who foretold the great affliction upon Jewry, which was to begin with the Babylonian captivity and continue until ultimately they would be dispersed into all the earth, also foretold that they would become famed in "every land" even while they as a people are subjugated and put to national shame. He also then foretold of their ultimate regathering, after which they "shall not see evil any more." Speaking of the termination of God's national judgment upon Jewry, the prophet says:

"The Lord hath taken away thy judgments, he hath cast out thine enemy [the Turk?]: the King of Israel even the Lord, is in the midst of thee: thou shalt not see evil *any more*. In that day it shall be said to Jerusalem, Fear thou not: and to Zion, Let not thine hands be slack. . . . I will gather [not every Jew, but] them that are sorrowful who are of thee, to whom the reproach of it was a burden. Behold, at that time [the "set time"] I will undo all that afflict thee: and I will save her that halteth, and gather her that was driven out; and I will get them *praise and fame in every land* where they have been put to shame." (Zeph. 3: 15-19.) In similar vein did Isaiah declare: "The Gentiles shall come to thy light . . . the abundance of the sea shall be turned unto thee; the *wealth* of the Gentiles shall come unto thee." (Isa.

60: 3, 5.) While these prophecies may have a spiritual fulfilment, yet they are having a literal fulfilment also, in God's providential dealings with His people Israel.

Successful as Tillers in the Holy Land

It has been declared that there is one field in which Jews do not excel, namely, in agriculture. It has been said that as a people they are "land-shy" and "city-mad." It is true, of course, that in America not much more than 1.5 per cent of the Jewish population is engaged in farming, while 98.5 per cent are city dwellers. That perhaps is because they find they can make greater fortunes in other pursuits than in American agriculture. But in Palestine fully a fourth of all Jews who have gathered there are settled in farm communities. Dr. Weizmann writes:

"Thousands of young Jews and Jewesses arrive here who have been tied to the apron strings of their native cities. They could not distinguish a hoe from a spade. Yet they have turned to the arid land of Palestine and have wrenched from it the secret of plenty and prosperity. Why is this? Why is the Jew now doing in the Holy Land what he was never known to do in other lands? Because he works under the inspiration of inherent and natural love for this land, which centuries of wanderings by his progenitors have not killed. Each of his movements is spurred by a feeling that this land is his own, by all the rights and traditions of civilization and Biblical teaching. The Jew tills the soil of Palestine with far more fervor than does the farmer of other countries. Because of this the Jewish National Home is making such remarkable strides in its agricultural development. This ardor, born of a long denied heritage, coupled with the introduction of modern equipment and scientific methods, is causing the land of Palestine to yield her increase."

Non-Jewish Interest in Zionism

The interest that Gentile peoples as well as Jews have taken in the present rehabilitation of Palestine seems significant; further pointing to the fact that the "set time" for a change of tenancy in the Holy Land has come, and that divine power is being exercised to speed the transition. First came the Balfour Declaration of 1917, heretofore mentioned, manifesting Great Britain's readiness to aid in the fulfilling of Israel's desire in such an undertaking. That historic official pronouncement said:

"His Majesty's government views with favor the establishment in Palestine of a national home for the Jewish people, and will use its best endeavors to facilitate the achievement of that objective; it being understood that nothing shall be done which will prejudice the civil and religious rights of existing non-Jewish communities in Palestine, or the rights and political status enjoyed by the Jews in any other country."

This British declaration was immediately endorsed by the principal allied powers, and also embodied in the Treaty of Sevres, wherein it was provided that Palestine should be entrusted to a mandatory power, the mandate to be approved by the League of Nations. A few years later Great Britain was given the mandate over Palestine by the League of Nations (1922), since which time the rebuilding of Zion has been permitted to go forward. Although the United States of America is not a member of the League of Nations, yet it manifested its interest in and approval of the British declaration, the U. S. Congress adopting unanimously a resolution endorsing the movement to reestablish in Palestine a Jewish National Home. Furthermore, in 1932 various Gentile leaders of Washington and elsewhere formed the Pro-Palestine Federation of America, to assist in the realization of Jewish aspirations in the rebuilding of their ancient homeland; and many American Gentiles have individually contributed money to the various Zionist funds as well as to this Pro-Palestine Federation.

Generous Support From American Jewry

But, as might have been expected, the great factor that is principally responsible for the rapid rebuilding of Palestine in recent years is the generous financial support that has come from Jewry in America. The Jews of Europe have indeed done their part, but as a class the Jews of the United States are far more prosperous than are their brethren over seas. Fully half of the $200,000,000 that already has been expended or invested in Palestine, either privately or under direction of the World Zionist Organization, has come from the pockets of Jews living in America.

Although Zionism did not originate in America, it was not long after its founding until it crossed the Atlantic and gained a firm foothold here. It was in 1898 that the Zionist Organization of America was founded, being then called "The Federation of American Zionists." Prof. Richard Gottheil, of Columbia University, was its first president, and Dr. Stephen S. Wise was its first secretary. Ere long there came to its support many other distinguished American Jews, such as Dr. Judah L. Magnes, who later became chancellor of the Hebrew University in Jerusalem; also Louis D. Brandeis, now Associate Justice of the Supreme Court of the United States; Judge Julian W. Mack, Nathan Straus, Louis Lipsky, Morris Rothenberg, Felix Warburg, and many others of like calibre.

Nor have the Jewish women of America neglected to do their part. On the contrary, in 1912, Miss Henrietta Szold organized a women's Zionist organization, called "Hadassah," which has dedicated itself to safeguarding the health of Palestine settlers. Today an elaborate hospital and clinic system exists in Palestine, also child welfare centres, nurses' training schools, medical laboratories, milk stations and playgrounds, all due to Hadassah. Furthermore, this women's organization is enrolling Jewish mothers, who are committed to the task of instilling the Zionist spirit and ideals into their children, thereby assuring a steady increase in Zionist ranks for the future.

The Land Being Bought, as Jeremiah Foretold

Although every phase of the rehabilitation work in Palestine is under the general direction of the World Zionist Organization, yet the expenditures are not made from one general fund; there are various funds, each concerned with its own particular field. For example: The Jewish National Fund provides for the purchase of land for Jewish settlement and cultivation. All land being taken over for Jewish settlement is being paid for. It was not God's intention that when the "seven times" of Israel's chastisement had ended, that Jews should attempt to seize or confiscate the land, even though it is their rightful inheritance. On the contrary, the land should be bought, so that no injustice may be done to the former occupants. Says the prophet Jeremiah, concerning this regathering of God's chosen people:

"Behold, I will gather them out of all countries whither I have driven them in Mine anger, and in My fury, and in great wrath; and I will bring them again unto this place, and I will cause them to dwell safely . . . as I have brought all this great evil upon this people, so will I bring upon them all the good that I have promised them. And fields shall be *bought* in this land. . . . Men shall *buy* fields for money, and subscribe deeds, and seal them, and take witnesses, in the land of Benjamin, and in the places about Jerusalem, and in the cities of Judah, and in the cities of the mountains, and in the cities of the valley, and in the cities of the south."—Jer. 32: 37-44.

Therefore it is the function of the Jewish National

Fund to make purchases and improvements of Palestine land, and already over $16,000,000 has been raised and expended for this purpose. This fund was founded under a provision which requires that two-thirds of the land purchased by it shall never pass out of the control of the Fund. Not only would it violate this provision to resell any of this land to non-Jews, but it cannot be sold even to Jews; the Fund must retain title to it; and it is then leased to individual Jews for a period of 49 years. Not only does the Fund make purchase of the land, but part of the Fund is also used for irrigation, drainage, clearing away rocks, and other needed improvements.

Systematic Jewish Colonization

The Keren Hayesod is a fund founded in 1920, since which time it has raised and expended about $25,000,000 for colonization purposes. In short, this fund takes up the work where the Jewish National Fund leaves off. After the land has been purchased and cleared of rock, or swamps drained, the actual settlement of the land and its cultivation must then be financed. This is the function of the Keren Hayesod. It establishes public works, conducts experimental stations, promotes education, encourages immigration, develops urban centres, and aids marketing. Then there also is the Hadassah, already mentioned, whose fund attends to hospitalization, and promotes general welfare. By having these separate funds, not only can each phase of the rebuilding work be promoted more expeditiously, but contributors are thereby enabled to make selection, and thus may have their money used in the particular department in which they are most interested.

Jews who settle in Palestine become citizens of this **Jewish commonwealth.** But a scheme has now been put into effect whereby any Jew who is interested in the rebuilding of this Jewish Homeland may be registered as a citizen thereof. In Jerusalem is kept a "Book of Remembrance," and in which is written the name and address of every Jew who contributes $100 or more to the Jewish National Fund. All whose names appear in this book are automatically made citizens of the Jewish Homeland. A few months ago the National Conference for Palestine assembled in Washington, D. C., and a nation-wide effort was launched, known as the United Palestine Appeal, having for its objective the raising of $3,500,000 in the United States. Similar efforts are being made simultaneously in other countries; and many Jews who heretofore have stood aloof from the Zionist movement are now rallying to its standard.

Never before have the prospects for the success of Zionism looked so bright as they do now. How can anyone longer doubt that the reason for this lies in the fact that God's due time has come to do for Israel all that He has promised He would do for them as soon as their "double" or national eclipse would end? That time has come; and nothing that man may do or fail to do could thwart the successful outworking of God's plan for His chosen people. The heart of every Jew should thrill at every present evidence that God is now extending His mercy to Zion, "even the sure mercies of David"; because "the time to favor her, yea the *set time,* is come!"—Psalm 102:13.

"**Comfort ye, comfort ye My people, saith your God. Speak ye comfortably to Jerusalem, and cry unto her, That her warfare is accomplished, that her iniquity is pardoned;**
For she hath received from the Lord's hand DOUBLE For all her sins!"—Isaiah 40:1, 2.

AMERICA AND THE HOLY LAND

An Arno Press Collection

Adler, Cyrus and Aaron M. Margalith. **With Firmness in the Right:** American Diplomatic Action Affecting Jews, 1840-1945. 1946

Babcock, Maltbie Davenport. **Letters From Egypt and Palestine.** 1902

Badt-Strauss, Bertha. **White Fire:** The Life and Works of Jessie Sampter. 1956

Barclay, J[ames] T[urner]. **The City of the Great King.** 1858

Baron, Salo W. and Jeanette M. Baron. **Palestinian Messengers in America,** 1849-79. 1943

Bartlett, S[amuel] C[olcord]. **From Egypt to Palestine.** 1879

Bliss, Frederick Jones. **The Development of Palestine Exploration.** 1907

Bond, Alvan. **Memoir of the Rev. Pliny Fisk, A. M.:** Late Missionary to Palestine. 1828

Browne, J[ohn] Ross. **Yusef:** Or the Journey of the Frangi. 1853

Burnet, D[avid] S[taats], compiler. **The Jerusalem Mission:** Under the Direction of the American Christian Missionary Society. 1853

Call to America to Build Zion. 1977

Christian Protagonists for Jewish Restoration. 1977

Cox, Samuel S. **Orient Sunbeams:** Or, From the Porte to the Pyramids, By Way of Palestine. 1882

Cresson, Warder. **The Key of David.** 1852

Crossman, Richard. **Palestine Mission: A Personal Record.** 1947

Davis, Moshe, editor. **Israel:** Its Role in Civilization. 1956

De Hass, Frank S. **Buried Cities Recovered:** Or, Explorations in Bible Lands. 1883

[Even, Charles]. **The Lost Tribes of Israel:** Or, The First of the Red Men. 1861

Field, Frank McCoy. **Where Jesus Walked:** Through the Holy Land with the Master. 1951

Fink, Reuben, editor. **America and Palestine:** The Attitude of Official America and of the American People. 1944

Fosdick, Harry Emerson. **A Pilgrimage to Palestine.** 1927

Fulton, John. **The Beautiful Land:** Palestine, Historical, Geographical and Pictorial. 1891

Gilmore, Albert Field. **East and West of Jordan.** 1929

Gordon, Benjamin L[ee]. **New Judea:** Jewish Life in Modern Palestine and Egypt. 1919

Holmes, John Haynes. **Palestine To-Day and To-Morrow:** A Gentile's Survey of Zionism. 1929

Holy Land Missions and Missionaries. 1977

[Hoofien, Sigfried]. **Report of Mr. S. Hoofien to the Joint Distribution Committee of the American Funds for Jewish War Sufferers.** 1918

Intercollegiate Zionist Association of America. **Kadimah.** 1918

Isaacs, Samuel Hillel. **The True Boundaries of the Holy Land.** 1917

Israel, J[ohn] and H[enry] Lundt. **Journal of a Cruize in the U. S. Ship Delaware 74 in the Mediterranean in the Years 1833 & 34.** 1835

Johnson, Sarah Barclay. **Hadji in Syria:** Or, Three Years in Jerusalem. 1858

Kallen, Horace M[eyer]. **Frontiers of Hope.** 1929

Krimsky, Jos[eph]. **Pilgrimage & Service.** 1918-1919

Kyle, Melvin Grove. **Excavating Kirjath-Sepher's Ten Cities.** 1934

Kyle, Melvin Grove. **Explorations at Sodom:** The Story of Ancient Sodom in the Light of Modern Research. 1928

Lipsky, Louis. **Thirty Years of American Zionism.** 1927

Lynch, W[illiam] F[rancis]. **Narrative of the United States' Expedition to the River Jordan and the Dead Sea.** 1849

Macalister, R[obert] A[lexander] S[tewart]. **A Century of Excavation in Palestine.** [1925]

McCrackan, W[illiam] D[enison]. **The New Palestine.** 1922

Merrill, Selah. **Ancient Jerusalem.** 1908

Meyer, Isidore S., editor. **Early History of Zionism in America.** 1958

Miller, Ellen Clare. **Eastern Sketches:** Notes of Scenery, Schools, and Tent Life in Syria and Palestine. 1871

[Minor, Clorinda]. **Meshullam!** Or, Tidings From Jerusalem. 1851

Morris, Robert. **Freemasonry in the Holy Land.** 1872

Morton, Daniel O[liver]. **Memoir of Rev. Levi Parsons, Late Missionary to Palestine.** 1824

Odenheimer, W[illiam] H. **Jerusalem and its Vicinity.** 1855

Olin, Stephen. **Travels in Egypt, Arabia Petraea, and the Holy Land.** 1843. Two Vols. in One

Palmer, E[dward] H[enry]. **The Desert of the Exodus.** 1871. Two Vols. in One

Paton, Lewis Bayles. **Jerusalem in Bible Times.** 1908

Pioneer Settlement in the Twenties. 1977

Prime, William C[ooper]. **Tent Life in the Holy Land.** 1857

Rifkind, Simon H., et al. **The Basic Equities of the Palestine Problem.** 1947

Rix, Herbert. **Tent and Testament:** A Camping Tour in Palestine with Some Notes on Scriptural Sites. 1907

Robinson, Edward. **Biblical Researches in Palestine, Mount Sinai and Arabia Petraea.** 1841. Three Volumes

Robinson, Edward. **Later Biblical Researches in Palestine and in Adjacent Regions.** 1856

Schaff, Philip. **Through Bible Lands:** Notes on Travel in Egypt, the Desert, and Palestine. [1878]

Smith, Ethan. **View of the Hebrews.** 1823

Smith, George A[lbert], et al. **Correspondence of Palestine Tourists.** 1875

Smith, Henry B[oynton] and Roswell D. Hitchcock. **The Life, Writings and Character of Edward Robinson.** 1863

Sneersohn, H[aym] Z[vee]. **Palestine and Roumania.** 1872

Szold, Henrietta. **Recent Jewish Progress in Palestine.** 1915

Talmage, T[homas] de Witt. **Talmage on Palestine:** A Series of Sermons. 1890

Taylor, Bayard. **The Lands of the Saracen:** Or, Pictures of Palestine, Asia Minor, Sicily, and Spain. 1855

The American Republic and Ancient Israel. 1977

Thompson, George, et al. **A View of the Holy Land.** 1850

Van Dyke, Henry. **Out-of-Doors in the Holy Land:** Impressions of Travel in Body and Spirit. 1908

Vester, Bertha [Hedges] Spafford. **Our Jerusalem:** An American Family in the Holy City, 1881-1949.   1950

Wallace, Edwin Sherman. **Jerusalem the Holy.**   1898

[Ware, William]. **Julian:** Or Scenes in Judea.   1841. Two Vols. in One

Worsley, Israel. **A View of the American Indians:** Showing Them to Be the Descendants of the Ten Tribes of Israel.   1828

Yehoash [Bloomgarden, Solomon]. **The Feet of the Messenger.**   1923